KNOWLEDGE
EXPERIENCE
AND ACTION

AN ESSAY
ON EDUCATION

KNOWLEDGE EXPERIENCE AND ACTION

AN ESSAY ON EDUCATION

HAROLD G. CASSIDY

Department of Chemistry
Yale University, New Haven, Connecticut

TEACHERS COLLEGE PRESS

Teachers College, Columbia University
New York

*T*his book is dedicated to Members of the Connecticut Science Teachers Association, whose efforts over the years to improve teaching in Connecticut have been an inspiration to me.

Preface

In this book I present a statement of educational principles, some of which have been forgotten, or not learned; some of which need restatement, even reinterpretation.

Education exists in tension between variety and constraint. Variety in courses, opinions, behavior, holds open the possibilities of change, allows for choice and for individual enterprise, and is dangerous if taken as an end in itself. Constraint, too, is dangerous as an end in itself. Yet it is essential that we have a firm basis of agreed premises. These—beliefs, axioms, postulates, faiths —hold our culture together and permit us to communicate meaningfully with each other. They are our inner fortress. There is every reason why this tension should be as creative as that between function and form, and all the other great creative, sustaining tensions of life.

There is, it seems to me, increasing emphasis on the irrational in certain areas of the Humanities—a type of anti-intellectual revolt. This is clearly on the side of variety, and indeed has its uses: new insights and intimations may emerge in this way; and the irrational does give meaning to the rational. At its best it can be a kind of catharsis, clearing away old and outworn forms to make place for new. A more constructive emphasis is on the nonrational component of wisdom: intuitive, highly subjective, and subject to its own laws, as the irrational is not. It "has its own reasons that reason does not know." But we must emphasize reason. It, too, is a source of insights, intimations, revelations, as well as the more formal, logical deliverances, and these, too, may be good or evil, true or false. Reason offers us the possibility of prediction and control of our habitat. Reason has been hard-won over the centuries of man's evolution, and cannot be relinquished. Only, it too is not an end by itself.

My objective, then, is to present a framework which the student, teacher, administrator, may utilize to confirm his own intellectual home. The ethical problem of what ought to be is certainly subject to continual test (in the light of past experiences): we can ask of an education whether it makes the student a better person; whether it helps him to reconcile, and even fuse, private and public needs; whether it unifies knowledge and experience; whether it conduces to a live and self-correcting society. I try to suggest how an educational process may

viii

be designed to give affirmative answers to these questions. But I do not prescribe for anyone. I treat of sciences, humanities, philosophies, and technologies because, and to show that, they are all connected; because acts or thoughts in one may well bear on the others. Out of the vision of the whole, each person constructs his own prescriptions.

This book is written for teachers, and for students planning to become teachers, and for laymen who are concerned with the state of our education and the quality of our lives, and whose children are considering college. These purposes are spelled out to some extent in Chapter 1 in connection with my justification for writing this book. In Chapter 2, I present the premises and largely undefended basic assumptions on which the rest of the book is built. This chapter provides a check list of premises relating to the natures of students and teachers; to knowledge, experience, and action; and to the educational process itself. Teachers and laymen alike, examining this check list, can see where I stand vis-à-vis themselves.

Chapter 3 is written to counter prevalent nihilism and to offer, through this brief essay on meaning, a basis for the optimism and enthusiasm that all teachers should have and show (most of the time!). Chapter 4 sets the context of the liberal education in holistic terms. Then Chapters 5 and 6 describe what I think the liberal arts education should do. I have included Chapter 7 because Coaction Theory is capable of providing the conceptual organizing framework for a liberal curriculum in connection with Chapters 5 and 6. It may be that details of the theory will have to be modified, but I think it is fundamentally sound and gives us the first real hope to subdue the fragmentation that has been destroying the liberal curriculum. Finally, in Chapter 8, I have tried to draw together what I have developed in the preceding chapters, and to present a philosophy of education and an approach to teaching and to choosing subjects that will, I hope, encourage teachers and help solve some present serious problems.

I am indebted to many persons and institutions. The Center for Advanced Studies at Wesleyan University, under the direction of Paul Horgan, gave me the time and encouragement to finish this work, begun at Yale in the midst of active teaching and research. Grants from the U.S. Public Health Service and Research Corporation kept my chemical research going and relieved me of much worry. One of the most important aids was a five-year grant by the Carnegie Corporation of New York to Dean William C. DeVane of Yale College. This enabled him to support me (among others) in experimental approaches to teaching science to nonscience and antiscience students. The experiences I gained in these years have borne fruit in the form of a textbook of physical science for these students, now in press with Freeman, Cooper & Co., San Francisco. At the same time these experiences fortified me to speak out in this book. So I owe a double debt to the Carnegie Corporation.

Another important influence has been the members of the Connecticut Science Teachers Association by whom I have been inspired. I have dedicated this book to them for their efforts and successes in improving science teaching in Connecticut, and for the encouragement they have given me, culminating in the Third John Prymak Service Award, given me "for . . . exceptionally devoted and valuable service to his colleagues in Science Education in Connecticut."

Several appointments as one of the seminar leaders at the Danforth Workshop for Liberal Arts Education fortified me to keep at the work. I am indebted also to numerous persons who read parts or the whole of the text at various stages of its preparation. I name them with thanks but no implication that they are responsible for what is written here, unless I specifically mention it: Mrs. Ann Freemantle, Mr. Paul Horgan, Mr. and Mrs. James A. Munro, Dr. and Mrs. Michael Polanyi. I owe a special debt to Mr. Edward F. Haskell, to whose work most of Chapter 7 is devoted. We have worked together for nearly thirty years, during his grueling effort to develop Coaction Theory. He not only gave permission to report this work but gave this book critical reading and made many suggestions which have strengthened it, which I have acknowledged as best I can. Undoubtedly, as we have worked together, influences upon each other which are not capable of being sorted out are responsible for other features of the work.

I owe an especial debt to Kathryn Childs Cassidy who has given me unfailing support and encouragement.

What I said in dedicating my first volume on this subject to her remains true: "she practices what I preach."

The title of Chapter 8, namely "One Culture, Indivisible," was suggested by an essay, "The Sciences and Humanities," by S. M. Garn, in *Antioch Notes, 42,* No. 3, 1964, which was brought to my attention by Mr. C. M. Forbes. It is used with permission.

I acknowledge with thanks the labors of Mrs. Barbara Satton of the Center for Advanced Studies, and Mrs. Mildred Ross Bray, at Yale, who typed and retyped for me.

I am indebted to the following persons and publishers for permission to quote them or use figures from their publications. From "A Country and Some People I Love," © Copyright 1965 by Katherine Anne Porter, September 1965 issue of *Harper's Magazine,* by permission of the author. From a review by Rebecca West in the February 1966 issue of *Harper's Magazine,* © Copyright 1966 by Harper's Magazine, Inc., by permission of the author; comments and figures from the work of Edward F. Haskell, privately printed or in scientific journals, by permission of the author. From "The Abdication of the Artist," by Paul Horgan, in the *Proceedings* of the American Philosophical Society, by permission of author and publishers.

The following publishers have kindly given me permission to quote from the cited works. American Sociological Association: Gwynn Nettler, in *Sociometry, 24,* 279 (1961). Harper & Row, Publishers: Eric Hoffer, *The*

True *Believer*, 1951; Michael Polanyi, *Personal Knowledge* (1964); Paul Ramsey, ed., *Faith and Ethics: The Theology of H. Richard Niebuhr* (1957); Chad Walsh, *From Utopia to Nightmare* (1962). Houghton Mifflin Company: Archibald MacLeish, from "Einstein" in *Collected Poems of Archibald MacLeish* (1926). The Macmillan Company: Alfred North Whitehead, *The Aims of Education and Other Essays* (1929). McGraw-Hill Book Company: Henry Margenau, *The Nature of Physical Reality* (1950). W. W. Norton & Company, Inc.: Martin Green, *Science and the Shabby Curate of Poetry*. Oxford University Press, Inc.: Arnold Toynbee, *An Historian's Approach to Religion* (1956). Princeton University Press: José Ortega y Gasset, *The Dehumanization of Art: And Notes on the Novel*, Helene Weyl, trans. (1948). Random House, Inc.: J. W. Goethe, *Italian Journey, 1786–1788*, W. H. Auden and Elizabeth Mayer, trans. (1962). Sheed & Ward, Inc.: Mircea Eleade, *Patterns in Comparative Religion* (1963). University of Texas Press: Roger J. Williams, *Free and Unequal: The Biological Basis of Individual Liberty* (1953).

H.G.C.

Contents

KNOWLEDGE
EXPERIENCE
AND ACTION

AN ESSAY
ON EDUCATION

1

Prologue

Here we are, inhabitants of a mass of rock, our nearly spherical Earth, the outer surface of which is crumpled and in good part covered with water. We live in a thin layer of this outer surface, a layer that contains a finite quantity of matter. Take a deep breath and the chances are high that you breathed in many nitrogen molecules breathed once upon a time by Cleopatra or Antony. This finite matter includes plants and animals, to the existence of which we are obligated for our continued life. Our planet spins in the ubiquitous glare of radio, heat, light, X ray, and cosmic radiation impinging from all about it. We are obligated in an absolute sense to our Sun for the energy which, traversing space in eight minutes from the boiling solar surface that expels it to the green leaf that absorbs it, makes possible photosynthesis and thus our own existence. We are here on "this precious little Space-Ship Earth" [1], come "from God-Knows-Where; . . . going to God-Knows-Where" [2]. We are on and of the Earth, and there is no physical escape.

The detailed, empirical knowledge of these facts, partial and fragmentary as it is, has all come to us through science, and largely within the last three hundred years or so. Before this, for the most part, one speculated; now we think that we have firmer knowledge. I say that we *think* that we know, for I believe that we must always leave an intellectual door ajar to admit the visit of the unforeseen. And this knowledge leaves us feeling as exposed as the most primitive man.

We must suppose that preliterate man felt these intimations of mystery and bondage. The ancient sovereign divinities all had mysterious powers to bind men; to demonstrate their sovereignty by showing man his impotence. Probably he withdrew into the immediate problems and daily duties of his existence, as we do, to escape the pressure of such thoughts. But whenever, in moments of reflection, or in the midst of inconsequent turmoil, these ideas come home to us, we must grapple with them. We must ask ourselves, and others, questions that, urgent to us, are still ageless: "What is a human being?" "What ought he to be?" "What dost thou in this living tomb?" [3].

These questions have no permanent absolute answers—and yet we must answer them, because we have to live, which is to act, in their light whether we are explicit about it or not. We turn to the words, songs, and art of wise men who have suggested answers; we listen to the words, songs, and art of contemporary claimants for that honored title. Sometimes in our need for assurance we forget that there are no absolute answers to these questions—only approximate answers. But, as Haskell emphasizes, permanence must be neither contrasted nor equated with precision. Many Biblical and other ancient answers contain permanent eternal truths. The answers are approximate; they become better approximations through the approach described in Chapter 7, and we might hope for still better approximations to ultimate (theoretical but unreachable) answers in future formulations. Yet the answers contain permanent, eternal truths. What plagues us is the problem of idioms. Every age has its own idiom. The beautiful language of the King James Version of the Bible avails nothing to the person who has not been brought up close to its imagery, so that he can translate its lessons into modern phrases. The child who is not taught the language of science is permanently maimed in this modern world.

I have risked the crudity of plain statement, and I continue, with some exaggeration, in the endeavor to make my point. Members of the intelligentsia—who merit the name because they concern themselves with these problems—have reacted to these questions in several different ways. Fundamentally, these responses are limited in number and new only in a quantitative sense.

There is the response of negation. The whole business is absurd, and thus each man must fend for himself. There are temperaments to which this approach is attractive, although it turns out to be basically unworkable: we do actually live among others; we may all actually gain more in communion with others than the sum of that which each contributes.

There is the response which dismisses such questions as meaningless, because we cannot devise ways of stating them quantitatively, of measuring them. This is a strong response for clearly if, according to one's theory, something does not exist one would be a fool to go looking for it. No one has proposed an expedition in search of the Snark. Not looking for it, one would be safe from the risk of disturbing the self-fulfilling theory. But the intransigent human mind, given to wayward thoughts that intrude themselves unbidden, still raises these "meaningless" questions, and it turns out that the theory which says they are meaningless can maintain consistency only under the most rigorous discipline: it must exclude questions that do not fall under its rubric, no matter what.

There is the authoritarian approach which says that answers to these questions *have* been given by certified wise men. We need only listen to them, interpret if we really must into our own idiom, and obey. But the modern person, whose ancestors made the Renaissance, has come pretty far from the state of mind that fully accepts such an approach. Granted that it may lay before one

4

all that is good out of the past. But only if this is offered not as something coercive and prescriptive, for much dross may also be thus offered, but as a starting point, can it be thankfully received.

Another response has been to reject everything, everything possible whatsoever, that comes to us on authority from the past. Thus a reaction against the rigidities of nonadapting dogmas has led to the opposite extreme: to intellectual childishness and naïveté, where the discovery of some idea (old, well known, and subtly explored in the knowledge and experience of a cultured person) is treated as a great new thing: an exhibition that is unfastidious, fatuous, pretentious. The outcome of this approach is that its practitioners lack standards: anything is possible. They do not have even the mythic safeguards of a primitive person. They are easily drained.

There is also, and finally, in this list, a response which is tentative, moderate, unconvinced yet seeking conviction. I believe that this response is widespread. Its proponents are neither shrill and hysterical, nor resigned and apathetic, nor alienated. They have their own passion for lambent answers. The spirit that shines through their response—Socratic in origin, I suppose, trained in the harmonizing tradition of Christian stress on humility, the subduing of pride, cooperation, and empirical tests of truth with emphasis on practice ("by their fruits ye shall know them")—is one of acceptance coupled with assertion. These questions *do* have approximate answers. We do know that we have ineffable thoughts. Yet the ineffable of today becomes spoken tomorrow when some genius says it. And the ineffable residue is not lessened; it is enriched. So with partial answers. Therefore we must be men, and continue the struggle. But we must carry it on in the light of past knowledge and experience, of present reason, of present new insights, of rational constraints that leave open the way for irrational nudges and intuitions. Further, the struggle is a process that is not steadily in one direction; it is far from neat, it is the result of action, retro-action, error and its correction; and it is carried out in the conviction, passionately held, that this is the only response becoming to a *human* being.

In this bald way that throughout does less than jus-tice to the complicatedness of actual cases, I have tried to sketch a state of affairs that has led me to write this book. Turbulence is the modern modality. Disoriented from the old patterns of life we may feel that we have no stable frame of reference upon which to construct our lives; and upon which to build the responses to life that we try to teach our children. I offer in the following chapters a view of the scene—withdrawn in order to re-establish its integrity. I state principles to which most people will adhere, propositions with which they will commonly agree. We *do* have a framework. I argue that we are all engaged, in the educational process, in trans-mitting tested meaning (the function of study and teach-ing), and in learning to find new meaning (research and teaching). I define meaning, and try to keep our feet on

6

the ground while reaching for the stars. I try to show that the way of balance—the final one of the types of response I have described—is also the way that yields greatest meaning and integrity in our lives, our culture, our world view. I equate this balanced approach to the ideal of the liberal arts, and show what these are that they deserve our praise and support. And I try throughout to "articulate breadth with incisiveness" [4]. But I do not prescribe for anyone. I hope to encourage thoughtful teachers who may already practice the liberal arts. I hope to rally them to each other in adherence to its standards, and in opposition to the divisive cults of specialization which, *apparently* successful in graduate school, are forcing themselves upon us in the undergraduate areas.

NOTES

1 "This precious little Space-Ship Earth" comes from Kenneth E. Boulding and Henry Clark, *Human Values on the Spaceship Earth* (Council Press, National Council of Churches, New York, 1966).

2 The quotation "from God-Knows-Where; . . . going to God-Knows-Where" is from the last stanza of the poem "Wilderness" by Carl Sandburg in *Selected Poems of Carl Sandburg*. Edited by Rebecca West (Harcourt, Brace & World, Inc., New York, 1926).

3 *"What dost thou in this living tomb?"* from Matthew Arnold, "Stanzas from the Grand Chartreuse," in *Poetical Works of Matthew Arnold* (Macmillan & Co., London, 1893), see p. 320:

> For rigorous teachers seized my youth,
> And purged its faith, and trimm'd its fire,
> Show'd me the high, white star of Truth,
> There bade me gaze, and there aspire,
> Even now their whispers pierce the gloom:
> *What dost thou in this living tomb?*

4 The phrase "articulate breath with incisiveness" is from an elegant essay by Martin Green, *Science and the Shabby Curate of Poetry: Essays about the Two Cultures* (W. W. Norton & Company, Inc., New York, 1965), cf. p. 75.

2

A Statement of Principles

The ideas of John Dewey, Alexander Meiklejohn, Alfred North Whitehead, and a few other writers on education, have so permeated our culture and so subtly influenced our ways of thinking about education that we are continually surprised at how modern they seem, and at how often an idea which seems new and interesting to us turns out to have sources in an earlier work. The surprise is, of course, only momentary, and perhaps partakes more of recognition than of anything else, for it stands to reason that what we do today is an outcome of our education. If these ideas were well implanted in our minds, and there connected to others, and to our observations, then it cannot be strange that when we try to communicate what we think of as our own ideas, because they come out of our own minds, they also express the thoughts that others contributed to our education. I have this kind of experience repeatedly, as I return to books I read, perhaps many years ago, books by Whitehead, Dewey, Ortega, Margenau, Meiklejohn, Northrop, Maslow, and a few others, to mention only recent and contemporary authors who themselves rest on the classics. It might even be asked, why then write on this well-discussed subject? The answer must be that what one so recognizes tends to be the most basic and unchanging aspects of knowledge, understanding, and wisdom; but interpretation changes with time and circumstances, and the exigencies of life require that living thoughts, firmly rooted in and nourished by these basic principles, yet mutate and express themselves in new ways. Thus it is necessary—one has the urge that cannot be denied—to state these in more modern idiom, with due response to new lights thrown upon them by new circumstances, and with new meanings that inhere in previously unobserved connections with other thoughts. A quotation from Whitehead [1] expresses a theme of this book:

> The students are alive, and the purpose of education is to stimulate and guide their self-development. It follows as a corollary from this premise that the teachers should also be alive with living thoughts. . . .

But it states the theme broadly: whole new sciences and arts have been invented since Whitehead and Dewey wrote. I do not think that these have changed the basic premises, but they certainly have changed some of the emphases. For example, improvements in some aspects of medical science based on improvements in systems-theoretic thinking (see below) have been so astonishing—particularly in respect of contagious diseases—that, with sanitation, antiviral agents, vitamins, and minerals, it almost seems as though death is an error on the part of the consumer, as Jerome Bruner puts it [2]. This has made a great change in the age distribution of our population, and thus has impinged on educational policies.

Psychological discoveries, particularly in the area of the persuasive arts, have potentially great impact on education, not only on improving the art of communicating that which should be learned, but also in the education that fortifies *against* the persuasive art. The implications of some of the discoveries about perception, and the way the brain functions; of the effects of psychotomimetic drugs; of electrode implantation; and of several other new techniques can hardly be foreseen.

But perhaps the most immediate and far-reaching effect on education comes from automation, which is part of cybernation, the technology of cybernetics. Automation is changing our culture so rapidly, in certain ways, that it will be only through the most strenuous efforts that we can maintain reasonable control of the situation. Such control as we can achieve must come through education, and we had better get at it. It is fundamentally the improvement in cybernetics (systems-theoretic thinking) that underlies the medical-sanitary improvements which have started the explosive chain reaction of population increase.

So the living thoughts that we must think, and the live students whom we must today teach, are in certain important respects different from those of Matthew Arnold's and Cardinal Newman's days—in some respects because of them, and of Dewey, and Whitehead, and many others—but in more numerous respects, perhaps, because events undreamed of by earlier educators have vastly changed the students' lives and their prospects. It is no condemnation to say that no one in 1880 could have predicted relativity, quantum theory, atomic fission, atomic fusion, and a long list of things we take more or less for granted today: they might only have predicted "change." No one today will have predicted some of the surprises in store for us by the year 2000.

A list of assumptions, some implications of which support the body of this book, is presented below. This list bears on various components of educational processes, as well as of educational institutions. A preliminary word may be said here on the matter of institutions. An educational institution is in the best sense the concrete embodiment of an ideal of life. The particular ideal of the college is that of an education which, tripartite, consists of study, teaching, and research, all interlinked, and in some cases hardly distinguishable. Other educational institutions, such as primary and secondary schools, also embody this ideal of life—but usually with much less emphasis on research. There are, of course, other ideals of life, embodied in institutions appropriate to them. For example, there are community, national, and world governments which embody the governance of communal life; marriage and the making of a home, which embody the freedoms of family life; institutions of law and medicine, which embody ideals of legal justice and medical healing; the church, which embodies what Toynbee called essential counsels and truths, valid to all times and places (as well as nonessential practices and propositions); and many other institutions. Every institution functions by the establishment of a context, or field, which by itself does nothing. Only in the interaction of this field, or milieu, with persons, can this field be shown to exist, and only thus can an observable effect— the outcome, say, of an educational process—be invoked.

What I mean can be shown by the following analogy: Suppose we have a metal bar. We have no way to tell by just looking at that bar whether it is or is not a magnet. The way to find out is to make a test: if it is, some other magnet will attract or repel one end, if brought close to it; iron filings will line up "in the field" of the magnet. We say, *on the basis of these inter-*

FIGURE 2.1 A bar of metal, said to be a bar magnet.

actions, that there is a magnetic field; that the bar is a magnet. So no institution can be said to *be,* except in its interactions; in the processes associated with it; in its orderly relationships.

Thus it is not enough to organize an institution. It must speak to the condition of someone, so that the interaction characteristic of it may be engendered. We are therefore concerned with a total process: with the natures of student and teacher; with the knowledge that is taught and the experience, understanding, and wisdom that are encouraged; and with the nature of the educational process, and institution.

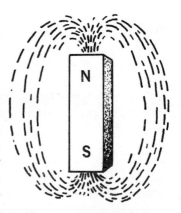

FIGURE 2.2 Iron filings lined up in the field of a bar magnet. Evidence that the bar of Figure 2.1 is a magnet by the "lines of force" visualized with iron filings.

The principles with which we are concerned in this chapter are most conveniently dealt with in groups, the members of which seem to have a natural affinity. Thus we start with assumptions relating to the nature of student and teacher; proceed then to assumptions about the subjects taught in terms of their content of knowledge, experience, and action; and conclude with assump-

KNOWLEDGE, EXPERIENCE, AND ACTION

tions relating to the educational process. We would like to treat all three of these classes of assumptions together, at once, as a kind of *Gestalt,* that is, holistically, since they all overlap and interpenetrate. But discourse forces us to string words out, and we respond in the time-honored way by classifying, and by asking the reader to carry out the necessary synthesis in his own mind.

Assumptions Relating to the Nature of Student and Teacher

One of the most basic assumptions about the student or teacher is that, as Maslow has said, *he has an intrinsic, biologically based, unchanging inner nature, in part unique to him and in part characteristic of our species.* This inner nature may be studied by scientific methods to discover its properties. That the properties of this inner nature can be studied scientifically does give us hope. We do not throw up our hands in despair. Instead, we have recourse to hypotheses which open the possibility to testing. All of this particular section draws on Maslow's ideas.

This inner nature, says Maslow, seems to be either neutral or good. It needs to be fostered and encouraged if we are not to become prey to disabling psychic illness or unhappiness. It seems to be weak, compared to instincts, yet always pressing for actualization. It may be overcome by cultural pressures, by frustrations, pain, tragedy, and wrong attitudes; or, these vicissitudes may reveal, challenge, and lead us to fulfill our inner nature in the face of the experiences of life [3]. Neutral or good (or bad) describes the relations of the inner nature to its habitat and to circumstances. Consider the analogy of the magnet: is the metal bar a magnet or is it not? Nothing intrinsic in it in isolation tells us this. Only if the habitat is changed by bringing up another magnet or some iron filings can we tell. A system is involved. I shall discuss this later, but the point is extremely important. Certainly there is an "innate" property of the metal bar that makes it a magnet: that it is iron and not silver, for example. The "intrinsic" structure of the metal atoms is important. We find out what this structure is by the methods of science, and these always involve interaction between entity and habitat in a systems-theoretic approach. You cannot look at a man and say he is good. His *behavior* is good, or neutral, or bad, and this can be assayed in his interactions with specific habitats in certain circumstances. From the outcomes of such observations one is at liberty to postulate an inner nature, but if it is called "good" or "neutral" or "bad," the terms should in some way be qualified, because they are not attributes of actions in that use.

I have included this hypothesis in hope, but with some misgivings. There is considerable evidence that different people see the world quite differently; that, as Gwynn Nettler [4] puts it: "bad people see the world differently from good." In a discussion of the attitudes and assumptions that underlie the equation of evil with illness, he asks, "What if evil is a way of responding to an imperfect world by actors with limited resources in a determinate situation?" And he continues, farther on, "we may have to choose between the 'health' of the man who behaves badly because he sees accurately and the 'health' of the man who behaves nicely because he has learned the popular ways of seeing falsely."

This question, and the answers given to it, are obviously of the utmost importance to education. Part of this importance is implied in the next assumption. But before leaving this one, I must remark that even if one finds in a study of laborers, bankers, or clerks that more than half are dishonest (some reports are quoted by Nettler) this does not mean that dishonesty gains sanction as a way of life: the matter is not subject to majority vote, it seems to me. Education is a tool which we use to fight the degrading forces that if left unchecked would destroy social and other life. The battle is continuous. The assumption which I have taken from Maslow, when made in operationally constant, cybernetic terms, is consistent with a postulated innate property which has made possible the gains we have made in pursuing honesty, truth, and clarity. Granted that much of the time we have reason to acknowledge only a little progress. But things did not *have* to be this way. The appearance of good behavior does have implications that support this assumption, or something like it. We do

A STATEMENT OF PRINCIPLES   17

have a basis for striving to maintain life against the randomizing forces that are checked, and subdued, only with living effort.

The student and teacher do not exist in isolation. Each is coupled to what may be named his habitat—which means the totality of all that affects him and that he affects. But contrary to classical notions, and as an outcome of Einstein's special relativity theory, there are parts of the universe that cannot be shown to affect him. As an extreme illustration of this naturally occurring constraint, it must be expected that the present state of a star one thousand light years distant can have no relation to the Earth or anything on it. We do not even know whether the star still exists. It might well have exploded. No news of its present state can reach the Earth for a thousand years. There are constraints, then, that set limits to the habitat.

It is evident that the habitat bears powerfully on the fulfillment of our inner nature. It may suppress completely, or actuate creatively, or support degrees of both. This habitat comprises persons, other living creatures, and things. There are, as parts of it, other students, other teachers, other administrators, our families and friends. And it comprises the design and upkeep (cleanliness, and so forth) of classrooms and laboratories, of buildings, of landscape; our home, and so on.

Whatever we do, good and bad, records itself in our unconscious. It "registers," as Karen Horney [5] describes "this unconscious perceiving and remembering." This being the case, we are obligated to ourselves and others to do the best we can with our life. Edward F. Haskell interprets the theologian's "sin against the Holy Spirit," the unforgivable sin, as ignorance of our own ignorance. Humility, he says, is our hedge against this sin. It seems to me that doing the best we can with our lives requires us to be at the same time aware of our ignorance and humble. We must learn to live with the insecurity of knowledge which has replaced to a large degree, and in other ways supplemented, the security of faith. We need faith, and reverence for life is our ultimate act of faith. Doing the best we can with our lives requires alert, subtle, humble self-making and self-changing [6].

The reader who wishes to pursue the psychological and other consequences of these postulates, together with the supporting evidence for them, should read Maslow and the references given by him that seem pertinent. I would myself urge each teacher to read Maslow and to ponder on his own consequent insights.

Assumptions Relating to Knowledge, Experience, and Action

Throughout this book I shall use the terms knowledge and experience to encompass that which is the province of education. Broadly speaking, knowledge comprises more of the intellectual side of education, with more emphasis on the cognitive, while experience comprises the more personal, subjective, intuitively apprehended side. Knowledge tends to be found in books; experience in "life," or "living." There is obviously knowledge about experience: nearly all scientific writing purports to convey knowledge about experience; the experience, here, is that which comes in considerable part from observing natural phenomena, and doing experiments. Nearly all critical writing in the Humanities, art criticism, literary criticism, history, and so on, convey knowledge about experience. Here the experience is that of the particular works: the paintings, sculpture, poetry, drama, novels, documents, that speak more or less privately to the reader, or viewer, or listener. One way of putting this matter is that you have knowledge "about"; you have experience "of" [7].

But anyone who has been involved with these things knows that the matter is not as simple as this. The two cannot be set apart as classes which are mutually exclusive. All knowledge has clinging to it some of experience, since *someone* apprehends the knowledge; correspondingly, almost all experience must have some component of knowledge adhering to it because we who have the experience are pattern-forming creatures: we like to, or have to, or do, connect things. This gives them meaning, and such connections do surely have an intellectual component that may be claimed to be knowledge. We do not have here some kind of sharply defined opposed qualities, but rather, once more, a range of emphasis. Of few things in our education can we say that they are either knowledge or experience. For the majority, if someone asks if it is this or not this, we have to reply "yes, but . . ."; "it is mostly this, but there is present a component of that." Because we must in truth answer in this way is the strongest evidence for a unity throughout the field of education. This is a unity permeating the diversity, without lessening its remarkable variety, but knitting the whole together. Certain assumptions, then, may be made about knowledge and experience.

Dissymmetry creates some phenomena. This is one description of a well-recognized state of affairs, namely that a duality or bipolarity pervades all of nature. This consists, so to speak, of ranges, each bounded by two functional absolutes [8]. This is one way of looking at the matter. Some of these ranges are quite clearly quantifiable—as, for example, the temperature scale. This extends from absolute zero, which in principle is unreachable, but capable of accurate determination because there is a theory *and* a set of measurements that allows mathematical extrapolation to it, to the limit of heat, which is set by the nature of matter, the speed of light, and the mass-energy relation. These two bounding absolutes give meaning to the relative measurements along the range of the continuum. Other continua are far from quantifiable, such as those of Good–Evil, Beauty–Ugliness, Truth–Falsity, Sacred–Profane. But we nevertheless can navigate along the range between the unattainable absolutes, recognizing that every mundane judgment in the range is compounded of some of each quality that would reach its pure manifestation in the particular absolute; and we can envision the absolute if we have a theory that allows us to extrapolate to it. Thus some theories of beauty, of truth, of good, of evil permit such extrapolation and at the same time perform the function of providing in the identifiable but unattainable absolutes touchstones against which to try the metal of mundane actions. We shall pursue this matter explicitly elsewhere in this book, and keep it in mind throughout.

Truth does not contradict itself. Because phenomena are created by dissymmetry, a duality pervades all nature, as we said. For this reason it is possible to derive paradoxes that may yet be true within their limits. Thus one may conceive, in a certain sense, of a truth, with a small *t*, which seems unconnected to, or even at odds with, other small-*t* truths. Yet when intervening or mediating truths are found, then it no longer is isolated but is given meaning as part of a greater whole. We shall be concerned with this further. It is based on a far-reaching postulate that lies at the foundation of the Sciences. This follows.

There is an essential order of nature. This is a postulate that is instinctive to most people in our culture, and certainly it is an article of faith to practicing scientists. Without this postulate, science, as we know it, could not function. This postulate does not imply that we have "the word" about nature. Always there have been incautious souls who have impetuously

KNOWLEDGE, EXPERIENCE, AND ACTION

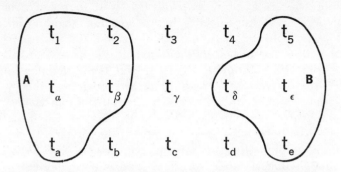

FIGURE 2.3 Small "t" truths are connected together. A person, *A,* having knowledge only of the truth looped together might well draw conclusions at variance from those of the person *B,* who has only the truths in his set. Both lack the connecting truths lying outside of their knowledge and experience. The situation is remedied as soon as the connections are found. The field of meaning of both *A* and *B* is thereby enlarged.

thought so, and even now, even after the shocks at the end of the last century and the turn of this, there are some who think that *now,* at last, we have the word. I heard one quite eminent scientist say that the quantum theory had now solved all chemical problems "in principle." Even with this "escape hatch" he must be wrong and guilty either of no knowledge of history, or of no belief in its lessons. For there was such a man, at the end of the last century, who thought physics was all finished—except for pushing back the significant numbers to the right of the decimal point by making ever more accurate measurements. He lived to see a conceptual mutation occur that shook the structure of classical physics. The foundations stood, but the superstructure had to be modified, and in the process of this modification brought about under the influence of Einstein's relativity and Planck's quantum theory, fantastic new knowledge and undreamed of experiences emerged. For nature is full of surprises, and I doubt if she has been exhausted by our efforts so far. At one time, as John Bevan put it, our world view was broad enough that nature's surprises were comprehended in the scheme as being supernatural. If this postulate says nothing about a supernatural it is because the possibility does not occur in science; but it cannot be excluded from a broader view, I think. No, the postulate means that were nature to present us, via some experimental results which were undeniably correct, with a fact that found no home in the structures of modern theory, we would believe, in the deepest meaning of belief, that this fact "makes sense." We would try to fit it into some kind of theory which also would comprehend the previously known undeniable facts. Some "facts" might turn out to be wrong, or wrongly interpreted, but we would confidently expect the foundations to stand firm.

One of my students, Richard Redpath, brought out the meaning of this postulate in a term paper. He had recently seen the play *Job* by Archibald MacLeish, and wondered what the plot would have been had Job been a scientist instead of the businessman that he was.

As he rewrote it, Job was tormented with variable laws, and irrational occurrences. Yet he kept on at his experiments, *believing* in an orderly universe as the reflection of a rational and just God.

"It is the scale that makes the phenomenon." This is quoted by Mircea Eliade [9], who continues:

> Henri Poincare queried with some irony whether "a naturalist who had studied elephants only under the microscope would think he knew enough about those animals?" The microscope shows the structure . . . of the cells . . . [which is] the same in all multicellular organisms. But is that all there is to know? At the microscopic level one cannot be certain. At the level of human eyesight, which does at least recognize the elephant as a phenomenon of zoology, all uncertainty departs. . . .

This extremely important principle is tacitly ignored in much teaching, not only in the realm of sciences but in all areas. Eliade points out how futile it would be to try to explain a work of literature by a list of social, economic, and political facts. Similarly, we shall stress the important holistic aspects of knowledge, experience, and action as they bear upon education: reductionism is to be discredited.

Neither the Arts nor the Sciences has a monopoly on any type of intellectual activity of which man is capable. By this I mean that creativity and inventiveness, logical reasoning, and subtle intuitions are found functioning throughout the areas of the Humanities, Sciences, Philosophies, and Technologies. This will be discussed further below. What distinguishes the Humanities from the Sciences, in these terms, are the kinds of subjects to which man applies these abilities. Scientists and scientific technologists generally are pretty choosy about the kinds of problems they undertake; they will attempt, for example, to work out the fantastically subtle and complicated problems of leaving the Earth and existing in outer space; to discover and control the physical, physiological, and psychological effects of weightlessness; and so on. But they tend, up to the present at least, to eschew problems relating to faith; to grace. Thus scientists tend to pick problems that are at least in principle soluble to the point of action and which will, it is hoped, present new, exciting surprises in the course of their solution. Everything else, including the subjective and the ineffable, are the province of the humanist: and here there may not be any answers of the same cogency.

When the Humanities, Sciences, Philosophies, and Technologies are brought together in a whole, functioning system there emerge ethical imperatives which confirm and extend the noblest ideals that mankind has collected and treasured. Put very briefly, this is related to religion; to the world view. Anthropologists tell us that when they come to know a human culture—no matter how primitive—they find that it is permeated and held together by a world view in which all happenings, acts of nature and man, rituals, cycles of birth to death of plants, animals, and men, are linked together in a meaningful whole. This is to say that the view is a sacred one. In a culture with such an all-encompassing world view we would not be understood were we to ask someone whether this or that facet were secular or sacred [10]. The entire culture is sacred. If, then, one pursues this farther, one finds, according to Toynbee [11], that all seven of the great religions are in agreement in certain respects. He says:

> In the heritage of each of the higher religions we are aware of the presence of two kinds of ingredients. There are essential counsels and truths, and there are non-essential practices and propositions.
>
> The essential counsels and truths are valid at all times and places, as far as we can see through the dark glass of Mankind's experience up to date. . . . In fact, the counsels and truths enshrined in the higher religions would appear to have still longer lives than the higher religions themselves. . . .

He continues,

> These accidental accretions [the non-essential practices and propositions] are the price that the permanently and universally valid essence [the essential counsels and truths] of a higher religion has to pay for communicating its message to the members of a particular society in a particular stage of this

society's history. We can express this in the traditional language of Christianity by saying that the price of redemption is incarnation.

What one observes, of course, is that these accidental accretions tend to become institutionalized. Whereas an institution should serve, one would think, for promoting the welfare of human beings, and therefore be capable of modification as the need arises, instead, "people who have identified themselves with it are prone to make an idol of it." Moreover,

> while institutional relations leave personal relations far behind in respect of the number of the souls that that they can bring together into society, all human experience testifies that institutional relations at their best cannot compare in spiritual quality with personal relations at their best.

It is often forgotten, too, that what might properly be called sacred are not things themselves (which might become idols) but *relations*. Now, things may stand as symbols, or signs, of relations, and so might be confused, in their use as media for communication, with the things symbolized—a common enough semantic error. This confusion is to be avoided in applying this postulate. Then it becomes apparent that the world view is a nexus of relations that confers meaning upon its parts. Science has something so clear to say here that I have discussed it separately, in Chapter 3.

Assumptions Relating to Growth

The individual person is in some very real and important sense unique, and the object of education. A liberal education is one that begins, continues, and enables the continued development of personal as well as intellectual life. The student's chief goal, in a way, is to master himself. The teacher has to make contact with the roots of the student's personality, as Joseph Katz [12] put it, to support him as a *person* while holding up to him unremittingly a high standard of possible *intellectual* achievement. For this mastery has personal and intellectual dimensions as well as social. However, it would seem that the student needs to achieve a sense of identity before he can develop intimacy. He has to compromise in some way between his physiological, psychological, and social development. The student may respond, if a teacher confuses his tasks with those that are the student's (quite properly), with "it's my life!" and with the implication that the teacher, the faculty, and indeed "all adults older than thirty, are wrong and not to be trusted." Yet by the nature of things the student in some ambivalent way needs the teacher for more than an instructor. He needs an example of someone who has achieved competence in an area; who displays integrity, and requires discipline toward the meeting of standards; who is an adult friend, but is not a relative.

I am not saying anything very new, here. In the last two decades or so there has been accumulating empirical, psychological, research-based information about the courses of development of children and adolescents, the one into the other, and they into young adulthood, that can tremendously improve teaching if it becomes understood, assimilated, digested, sorted for authenticity, and creatively practiced by teachers. There is some evidence, for example, that the student needs for his personal growth to achieve a sense of competence in at least some one area. This comes from being faced with problems that at least *he* can solve. Continued frustration is destructive of the personality. This is to say that there are differences in abilities and temperaments among students, and we need even more to recognize these and take account of them since we are requiring (or encouraging) more students to go to college while at the same time raising standards and crying an undifferentiated and even unanalyzed "excellence." The individual student, then, needs increasingly more attention.

No limit whatsoever may be put to the possibilities that can be materialized through man's inspiration, will, integrity, and intelligence. This belief is the basis of an optimistic approach to the solution of educational problems. In relation to the previous assumption it bears on the vigorous attempts now being made in several large colleges and universities to give more attention to the individual student. In some instances the student can still say (and I don't recall the source of this), "No one paid any attention to me until I bit my IBM card." But the situation is remediable: perhaps through quite novel approaches. It bears also, at another level, on the development of the disciplines themselves. This belief has unifying implications, for it says, as I have indicated elsewhere, that not scientists, nor humanists, nor philosophers, nor technologists, not any of them, has a monopoly on any type of activity of which men are capable. I see no picket fence around the Sciences that is posted against poets, nor any valid interdiction against the scientist's trying his tools on a problem in the Humanities—only, each should understand what he is doing if error, and damage due to incompetence, is to be avoided.

The search for truth is the act of free men, and it helps to maintain their freedom. Michael Polanyi [13] says:

> a free society accords both independent status and a theoretically unrestricted range to thought, though in practice it fosters a particular cultural tradition, and imposes a public education and a code of laws which uphold existing political and economic institutions.

This is something the importance of which the student needs to learn in the process of becoming a contributing member of society. It involves the difference between words and action. There is freedom and range to words, restricted only by the canons of good taste, which has more to do with form than content; but in the case of actions, other considerations enter. Most important actions are essentially irreversible, and thus the propriety of their evocation depends on being able to predict their effects; being able to judge their moral consequences; being, in short, *responsible* in undertaking action. This responsibility may be hard for the young-man-in-a-hurry to accept, even though the evidences present him with instances of men repenting at leisure the effects of actions taken without thought. Who was the character in a Dostoevski novel of whom it was said "he was young and abstract, and therefore cruel"? Michael Polanyi states this belief:

> *"I believe that in spite of the hazards involved, I am called upon to search for the truth and state my findings."* This sentence, summarizing my fiduciary programme, conveys an ultimate belief which I find myself holding. . . .

There are no single, permanent, complete, and universally applicable solutions to the complex problems of education. There may well be optimal solutions, but these must be so designed as to remain flexible, so that errors may be corrected, and so that evolution remains possible.

There is no reason why either the Humanities or the Sciences need conform to canons devised for the other. This is a matter of some importance in educational administration, for a neat-minded programmer may wrench the credits given to the one type of course to fit the other. In a laboratory course, for example, a great

32

deal of teaching may go on—but in quite a different context from that of the classroom. The latter may be highly theoretical; the former may be concerned with reducing the theory from wide generality to practice in the individual instance of a chemical test, or reaction; to a cell or tissue seen through a microscope; to a particular animal whose behavior is being studied. The two kinds of activity are incommensurable. The laboratory teaching cannot be equated to the ordinary classroom work in literature or history. It may, however, be approximated by a seminar.

"Any [scientific] subject can be taught to anybody at any age in some form that is honest." Jerome Bruner says that this was "one of the conclusions of the 1959 Woods Hole Conference of the National Academy of Sciences on curriculum in science." This assumption, *which may not be pushed too far,* I think, is likely to be true of some theoretical descriptive science and the applied sciences. It would obviously not apply to those serious disciplines that rely upon the psychological attitudes and emotional experiences that only begin to develop in adolescence: the sensitivity that is prerequisite to true understanding of much poetry, drama, the novel, and so on. Such sensitivity may also be requisite to the fullest entering into a science.

A function of education is: to transmit to us the meanings that have been found in life by our ancestors; to teach us how to find new meanings consonant with the growth and change of our culture so that we may control *that growth and change; to enable us to live with inconsistency without becoming fragmented; to nurture a sense of mystery in the face of life; to arm us in the acceptance of our ultimate limitations without rendering us incapable of action.*

In this function is united study, teaching, and re-search: research being the finding of new meanings that link the old traditions to new circumstances; teaching, the communication of meaning; and study, the mastering of these meanings. We are thus led to an enquiry about meaning.

NOTES

1 The quotation from Alfred North Whitehead is from the first paragraph of the Preface of *The Aims of Education, and Other Essays.* A Mentor Book (The New American Library, New York, 1949 [The Macmillan Company, New York, 1929]).

2 Jerome S. Bruner, *On Knowing: Essays for the Left Hand* (Harvard University Press, Cambridge, Mass., 1962), p. 55.

3 *Cf.* Abraham H. Maslow, *Toward a Psychology of Being.* (D. Van Nostrand Co., Inc., Princeton, N.J., 1962), pp. 3 to 5.

4 Gwynn Nettler, "Good Men, Bad Men, and the Perception of Reality," in *Sociometry, 24:279* (1961), pp. 280 and 281.

5 Karen Horney is referred to by Maslow.

6 Haskell's interpretation is a personal communication.

7 For a discussion of "knowledge about," and "experience of," see John Hospers, *Meaning and Truth in the Arts* (University of North Carolina Press, Chapel Hill, N.C., 1946), pp. 235 ff.

8 For a discussion of "absolutes" see Harold G. Cassidy, *The Sciences and the Arts: A New Alliance* (Harper & Row, Publishers, New York, 1962), especially Chaps. 7 and 11.

9 Mircea Eliade, *Patterns in Comparative Religion.* Meridian Books (World Publishing Company, Cleveland, Ohio, 1963 [Sheed and Ward, New York, 1958]), p. xiii.

10 For a discussion of the sacred society, see Eliade, above, and Edward F. Haskell, "The Religious Force of Unified Science," in *Scientific Monthly,* 54:545 (1942), and Laura Thompson, "Relations of Men, Animals, and Plants in an Island Community," in *Science, 108*:263 (1948).

11 Arnold Toynbee, *An Historian's Approach to Religion* (Oxford University Press, London, 1956), pp. 264, 266, and 268.

12 Joseph Katz presented the ideas referred to here in a general lecture at the Danforth Workshop on Liberal Arts Education, summer of 1965.

13 Michael Polanyi, *Personal Knowledge. Toward a Post-Critical Philosophy.* Harper Torchbooks (Harper & Row, Publishers, New York, 1964 [University of Chicago Press, Chicago, 1958]), pp. 214 and 299.

3

Aspects of Meaning

When, today, we hear the cry "Meaningless, Meaningless" raised in so many tones and accents, and applied to so much of life, we need more than ever to hold steadily to the old wisdom that *meaning resides in organized connectedness*: in organized connectedness as it is perceived, or imagined, or postulated on the basis of some theory, by one person or many. Those who, for whatever reason, preach the meaninglessness of existence do surely preach a self-fulfilling doctrine, for if one accepts the doctrine, then it is heresy to search for meaning, and thus meaning will not be found. This is a form of what Abraham Maslow [1] characterizes as "high I.Q. whimpering on a cosmic scale [that] occurs whenever an external source of values fails to work."

It is important to anyone concerned with education

to examine the nature of meaning, for part at least of education is to foster and transmit the meanings that men have found in their existence. We must therefore examine into some aspects of meaning as part of our broader concern with the field of education.

If meaning resides in organized connectedness—and I take this as axiomatic—then if there were an isolated object or idea, it would have no meaning, because unconnected. But I very much doubt that such an isolated object or idea could be found. Where would we look for an isolated object? Far, perhaps, from the homes of human beings? But even the smallest particle of cosmic dust is only relatively isolated at any instant of its journey through time and space as we imagine it; and the largest galaxy is no more isolated. Every world line intersects others. Connectedness is immanent in nature as is organization. Where would we find an isolated idea? I doubt if we could find one. For ideas originate in that fantastically complicated and interconnected organ, the brain, and cannot appear by themselves.

Granted, then, that nothing can be found that is *absolutely* without meaning in the sense of being absolutely without organized connections, we must at the same time admit that we are far from making connections between everything in our knowledge and experience. We are led therefore to visualize another of those extensive subtly graded and many-dimensional gamuts, or ranges, that stretch between two absolutes: from absolute meaning*less*ness, not attainable (because absolute) but approachable and therefore calculable by extrapolation from experience, to absolute meaning*fulness*, where all connections are made—this, too, equally unattainable, but indefinitely approachable. Between the two lie all of knowledge and experience: from the most trivial and nearly meaningless on the one side to the most profound and meaningful on the other. The relativity of intermediate positions along this continuum is quite obvious and, if this alone were seen, then indeed there might be cause for despair. But if the range is conceived, anchored on its two opposed temporal absolutes, even though these are unattainable and subject to evolution inexhaustibly, and the possibility that by human means one can move along it is recognized, then a sense of duty and reverence becomes possible: duty in the sense that we have "potential control over the course of events," as Whitehead [2] phrases it, "Where attainable knowledge could have changed the issue, ignorance has the guilt of vice"; and reverence in the sense referred to by the physicist Max Planck [3] as "a blessing for the human mind in its search after knowledge," that the goal is unattainable, and the struggle toward it unending.

Before looking at the implications for education of what we have said, it is necessary to suggest that organized connectedness—and therefore meaning—can come in many guises. Many names are given to the making (or finding) of such connections: integration, organization, patterning, development of schemata; and these may apply to objects, signs, symbols, concepts, actions.

"To be," says Whitehead [4], "is to be related." We are especially concerned with the making of organized connections at the intellectual level, but these cannot be divorced from the other kinds at other levels, since we are ultimately concerned with the totality of connections.

The reason for this ultimate concern may be stated in various ways. We might begin, for example, with the simple connections that we commonly see as similarities: this thing, idea, or act is like that one in certain ways, and therefore we can conceive it as a member of a class. But it has differences, too, which may put it, in these respects, into other classes. This individual belongs to the class of human beings. He is male, and thus a member of a subclass of human beings, and of the much larger class of animals and plants of which maleness is a classifying attribute. He is five feet, nine-and-one-half inches tall; he was born on October 17, 1906, in Havana, Cuba; he belongs to the restricted class of persons named Cassidy, the still more restricted class with the middle name Gomes followed by Cassidy, and to the class with probably one member whose full name is Harold Gomes Cassidy, with at the same time membership in all the other classes. George Boole [5], an English mathematician, and the inventor of the algebra of classes, or sets, pointed out a century and a quarter ago that the cumulated memberships in classes can characterize a single individual who fulfills all the requirements of membership in many classes if there are enough of them. Thus to classify need not be to remove individuality; it may, in fact,

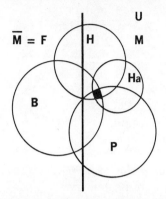

FIGURE 3.1 Example of a Venn diagram.

give meaning to the individual by showing his connectedness to others as a member of many classes.

For those who like to visualize these relationships in the form of pictures which can be grasped at a glance, there are the little diagrams which have come to be known as Venn's diagrams (though Leonhard Euler and other mathematicians also used them). We might diagram the example just given. Suppose that the set of all members, or *elements*, that we are considering is the set of all human beings. We call this the universal set, or *universe*, *U*. We choose it, and define it by some such statement as that used: "all human beings," or, if it were more manageable we might enumerate it, by giving a list of the members of the set. We similarly define this subset *M* of all males. (All the members of *U* outside of *M* would be "not-*M*," designated $\overline{M}$. In this case, females, *F*.) The class of people five feet, nine-and-one-half inches tall, *H*, is shown by the circle. The circle cuts both *F* and *M* because there are some females of this height. There is no attempt to make the area of the circle proportional to the number of these people. The people born on October 17, 1906, is *B,* and those born in Havana, Cuba, is *P.* Those people named Harold (all male) is *Ha.* Then the *intersection* of all these circles (the blackened portion of the diagram) represents the restricted number of people named Harold, who were born in Havana, Cuba, on October 17, 1906, are five feet, nine-and-one-half inches tall now. This is obviously a fairly restricted class. Further restriction is achieved by the two additional names, but the Venn's diagram circles are not drawn in because this would clutter up the diagram, which has already indicated the principle. In the algebra of classes, intersection is indicated by $\cap$. Thus the blackened portion represents the intersection of *M, H, B, P,* and *Ha,* and would be stated symbolically, $M \cap H \cap B \cap P \cap Ha$; and verbally, as "the class of entities (persons) who are at the same time members of the classes of male human beings, now five feet, nine-and-one-half inches tall, who were born October 17, 1906, in Havana, Cuba, and named Harold."

We might point out, too, that classification, and the special kind of classification that is known as quantitative measurement—putting the quality that is being measured into a class that is characterized by a particular number—is not necessarily a dehumanizing activity. If it were, then the teacher of art, or literature, or classics would be equally guilty with the teacher of mathematics, physics, or psychology, of dehumanization when he gives a numerical grade for an essay, or on an examination.

To rank degrees of quality is of the essence in giving meaning to the work, and to the student himself.

Perhaps the nicest demonstration of the use of quantitative measurement to display and support individuality, is to be found in the reports of the investigations of Professor Roger Williams [6]. He has drawn together a large number of data derived from easily measurable properties of body fluids and from other measurable quantities. These he has displayed in patterns, four of which are shown in Figure 3.2. The diagrams, all different, even for identical twins (the lower pair), support our knowledge based on quantitative data at a very basic, molecular level. How much more force is thereby given to the conviction of differences at more complex levels!

I have discussed classification at some length because it is one of the primitive and basic operations of almost any intellectual endeavor, and particularly because it exemplifies what I mean when I say that unity, union with other members of the same class, can be achieved without destroying variety or requiring uniformity, since membership in many other classes may characterize an entity—to the limit of certifying that it is unique.

Consider, then, the meaning that is conferred by what we might describe as operational, or functional connectedness. This is the kind of connectedness that elevates a collection of parts into a functioning whole—or a whole capable of functioning. The most simple of

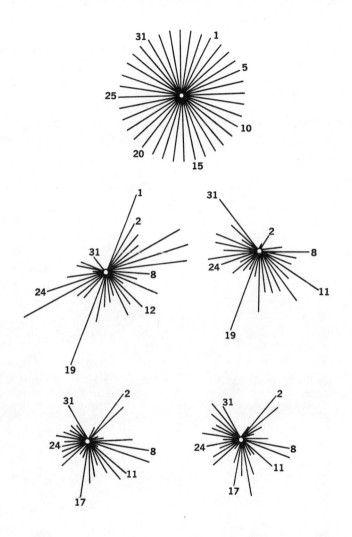

KNOWLEDGE, EXPERIENCE, AND ACTION

functioning wholes are machines, of one kind or another; more complex are nonhuman living organisms; still more so are human beings; and most complex of all are associations of human beings.

To make clear the increase in meaning that comes with increase in connectedness and organization, we might look first at classes of machines. In order to make the descriptions as general as possible, I will use the terminology introduced by de Latil [7] and his classification scheme, but with some omissions and paraphrasis.

FIGURE 3.2 Patterns of four individuals are shown, with an "average," the symmetrical pattern at the top. (From Roger J. Williams, *Free and Unequal: The Biological Basis of Individual Liberty* [University of Texas Press, 1953], pp. 109, 110; used with permission.) The successive numbered lines represent the items: 1–5, taste sensitivities for creatinine, sugar, potassium chloride, sodium chloride, hydrochloric acid; 6–17, salivary constituents: uric acid, glucose, leucine, valine, citrulline, alanine, lysine, taurine, glycine, serine, glutamic acid, aspartic acid; 18–31, urinary constituents: citrate, unknown base, unknown acid, gonadotropic hormone, pH, pigment/creatinine ratio, chloride/creatinine ratio; hippuric/creatinine ratio, creatinine, taurine, glycine, serine, citrulline, alanine. The lengths of the lines indicate values relative to the average, which is adjusted on a scale to give the symmetrical pattern shown at the top. (This legend is taken from *The Sciences and the Arts: A New Alliance* [Harper & Row, Publishers, 1962], p. 152.)

NOTE: The lower pair of diagrams were obtained from identical twins. Each figure is distinctive, but these are more alike than any other pair, indicating that heredity has something to do with the factors that these patterns measure.

Following de Latil's classification, the simplest artifact, not yet a machine, is a tool: something such as a hammer, or a lever. It is "a material [passive] extension which man gives himself in order to do something." Less simple is a first-degree effector. It executes a simple action under suitable stimulus. Examples are a typewriter key, or a hand brake, which utilize the principles of the lever but in some specified action. The effector is artificial, being created by man. The second-degree effector coordinates several first-degree ones, as in a clockwork, or a simple calculating machine. Most of what is classically called machinery belongs in this category. But when the effector is designed to act just in certain selected circumstances, as does an automatic fire alarm, then it must be advanced in the classification to the third degree. A still higher degree in the classification of effectors is reached when the machine is so designed that it will maintain and stabilize its own activity, as does a thermostatted heating plant, or an automatic pilot. Some machines have been designed to seek a goal, as set by the builder, but in so behaving they respond to stimuli and change their activities so as to reach the goal in spite of (limited) obstacles. Such machines, designated as fifth-degree effectors, have been designed by W. Ross Ashby, and others. Sixth-, seventh-, and eighth-degree effectors, which transcend mechanism, have been discussed by de Latil.

Michael Polanyi has discussed the relation of the machine to the nature of the materials of which it is made [8]. The machine is, on one level of reality, capable of description in physical and chemical terms. The materials of which it is made can be analyzed in great detail, chemically, and the shapes, motions, torques, and so forth of the working parts can be described in terms of physical theories. But none of these analyses will be able to tell whether the object of study is a machine, and if so, what it is to do, and how it is to do it. For this knowledge one must turn to the technology that applies the sciences, for here purposes are considered. (In the quotation from de Latil in the previous paragraph, the relevant words are "in order to do something.") This is another level of reality which, however, depends upon the former level. Thus, the proper functioning of the machine depends upon its being made of suitably strong materials with the right chemical and physical properties. But while these may have some meaning in themselves, as physical and chemical facts, they have no meaning for the nature of the machine. This more comprehensive meaning inheres in understanding the relations of the particulars in their organized connections into a coherent entity. This comprehension in terms of a coherent entity is a personal act, which is basic to Polanyi's theory of Personal Knowledge. We might recall, here, the statement in Chapter 2 that the scale makes the phenomenon.

Our point is, then, that with the organization of particulars into coherent wholes, for a purpose, there goes an inherent increase in meaning. This grows, expands, enlarges, with increase in the subtlety of the organization and the multiplicity of the connections. We shall show this with physical theory, below. And many new facets appear, to reflect the light of increasing meaning. This matter has been discussed in another way, but with essentially the same conclusions by David Bohm [9].

This discussion of machines, or effectors, as wholes of which the parts are connected in an organized way, was presented partly at the physical level: that of the things themselves. But there is a more general and in some ways more fruitful way of seeing the connections and organization. This is to conceive of the effectors in terms of their *behavior*, divorced from any particular physical embodiment. We speak, then, of *systems*, and with Ashby [10] define the system as a list of variables, the changes of which constitute *behavior*, and which may receive embodiment in many different ways. This important approach, which is fundamental to cybernetics, can be introduced most conveniently by starting in a relatively simple way.

We have already introduced Venn's diagrams. Suppose that we think of a class $\overline{P}$ which is characterized by a property p. Now, "property" is clearly another name for "behavior," as chemists and many other persons have recognized. For example, having the property of blueness is showing the behavior toward a normal eye, or a color-comparator, that the sky may show on a clear day; that is shown by the field on which are placed the fifty stars of the United States flag; by the petals of a Texas bluebonnet, or a forget-me-not; by the Yale Y on the Yale flag; by copper sulfate solution. If p is a statement of the property of blueness, then P is the class of things of which it may truthfully be said "p": that is, that they all show the property of blueness. We use the lower-case p for the statement, and the capital P as the name of the set, or class, of which the statement is true. We may have another class, Q, of each member of which it may truthfully be said "q"; that is, that each shows the behavior q (whatever it may be). Notice that even at this level of discourse, there is the hazard that we *may* make a wrong judgment. Thus we see recognizable values appearing.

Logicians have worked out relationships between statements which enable them to test, in a formal way, whether or not compound statements (connected in an organized way) are true or false, and to connect these to the algebra of classes. A very simple and elementary introduction to these logical methods is sufficient to carry us as far as we need to go along our way to the cybernetic notions. The three logical manipulations that are basic to the whole of logic and mathematics are those of negation, conjunction, and union. (Actually, only two may be needed, but three are more convenient.) Negation of a statement "p", is "not-p" (or "$\bar{p}$") and may be rendered "it is not the case that p." In our example, $\bar{p}$ is the property of not being blue, and everything that is not blue belongs in the class $\bar{P}$. If we take the circle $\bar{P}$ to represent the class of behavior of which it is true

to say p, a judgment that can only be made on the basis
of having a clear idea of the criterion of the class, that
is, blueness, and of *actually examining* each entity to
see if indeed it is blue, then everything outside of the
circle, of which it is relevant to say p, belongs to the
class $\overline{P}$. Now some of the entities of which it is true to
say "p" may also have the behavior of which it is true
to say "q". Of them it will be true to say "p and q," or
in the symbolic language, "$p \land q$". Of all the rest it
would be false to say "$p \land q$". We can therefore write
down the *truth-table* for the relation "*and*," or "*conjunction*," which is the technical name for the relationship, in the form:

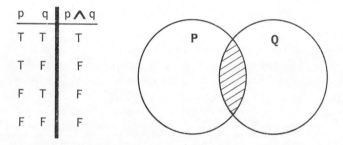

p	q	$p \land q$
T	T	T
T	F	F
F	T	F
F	F	F

FIGURE 3.3 Venn's diagram for the relation "and".

where "T" stands for true and "F" for false. Thus "p
$\land q$" is true only when both p and q are true. In the
Venn's diagram notation, the *intersection* of the P circle
with the Q shows the hatched portion of the two classes

50

for which "$p \wedge q$" may truthfully be said of the members: this is the class $P \cap Q$, as described above.

The third relationship is that of the statement "p or q or both", symbolized as $p \vee q$. This may also be stated "either p or q or both". The truth-table immediately follows:

p	q	p $\vee$ q
T	T	T
T	F	T
F	T	T
F	F	F

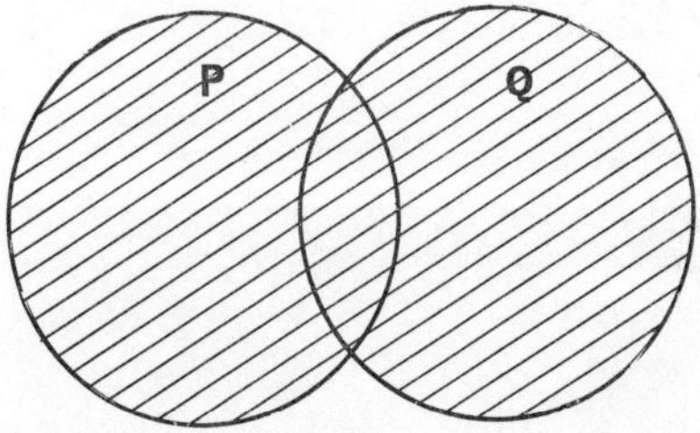

FIGURE 3.4 Venn's diagram for the relation "or, or both".

And the Venn's diagram for the *union* of the classes "P or Q or both", $P \cup Q$, is the hatched portion of the diagram that includes all of P and Q.

We have, in effect, been saying, so far, that "there is an object, or a behavior, or property, or whatever, that belongs to the class, or set, P, of which it is true to make the definite statement p." But we might wish to be less explicit so as to leave the question open—whether there are any members of a particular class with a stated relationship; indeed, the relationship may not actually be stated except in the most general, numerical form. Thus we might consider all the numbers, and enquire whether any of them fulfill the property stated by "*p*", that "$x^2 = 4$". Clearly, there are two: $+2$ and -2, and no others. We thus have as members of the class *P* the numbers $+2$ and -2 of which it may truthfully be said "$x^2 = 4$", when one or the other replaces x. We

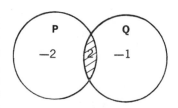

FIGURE 3.5 Solution of simultaneous equations.

may have another open statement about numbers which designates the property "*q*", that "$x^2 - x - 2 = 0$". The numbers that belong to the class *Q* of the members of which this statement is true are $+2$ and -1. Now, it follows that $+2$ is common to both sets, so that $P \cap Q$ is the set with the single member $+2$, about which it is true to say "*p* and *q*": and it follows that this is the solution of the two simultaneous equations. Of course, in an algebra class we would not normally draw Venn's diagrams to solve a set of simultaneous equations. We have easier ways of going about it. It is the connection between logic and algebra that we wish to show [11].

We have, therefore, a connection between logical statements and algebraic statements which is one small bit of evidence for the comment that symbolic logic, the calculus of statements and their relationships, is closely connected to mathematics. Our purpose in showing this is to make the connection between these two great bod-

KNOWLEDGE, EXPERIENCE, AND ACTION

ies of organized systems of symbols, with the intention of carrying the connections still further.

We have said that the relationships of logic and mathematics may be embodied in effectors; that we may adduce a *system*, the behavior of which represents the action of the effector. This becomes apparent all around us, if we look for it. Someone has said that every machine embodies the statement of a syllogism. Certainly, every machine may be represented by one or more—sometimes an inordinate number is needed—logical statements. To show how this is so, in principle, can be done in connection with simple electrical circuits. Suppose we have a simple on-off electrical switch (Figure 3.6).

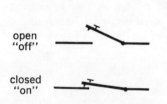

open "off"

closed "on"

FIGURE 3.6 Simple on-off electrical switch.

We let, in a quite arbitrary choice which, once made, we remain consistent to, the state, or property, or behavior "off" be represented symbolically by "F", and "on" by "T". Then we would say that if the statement p is "it is closed", and $\tilde{p}$ "it is open", we could say of the switch either p or $\tilde{p}$, depending on its state, *which we would have to examine.* Thus we have two classes of *behavior,* P (the closed switch) and $\overline{P}$ (the open switch). Now we introduce the switch into an electric circuit with batteries B and a light-bulb L, and have the essence of a flashlight and the embodiment of a logical relationship (Figure 3.7). We can see the difference between "on" and "off" because the bulb lights up when the switch is "on" and current flows.

Since it is only when a circuit is closed that the current can flow and light up the bulb, it follows that the relation of intersection of *P* and *Q* is readily shown with two switches connected "in series," while the relation of union is shown by switches connected "in parallel". But we said that all of mathematics could be generated by appropriate combinations of three relations, between statements. Since these are correlated exactly with sets, or classes, and the behavior of these can be embodied in these simple pieces of hardware, one can see, at least intuitively, that by combining these, and much more subtle pieces of apparatus *based* on these, one can embody quite complicated mathematical statements. It is through extensions of this idea that one arrives at computers.

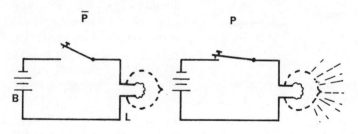

FIGURE 3.7 Embodiment of a simple logical relation in the form of a flashlight circuit.

Without pursuing these ideas any further, it is evident that the effector can, at least in principle, be given canonical representation in symbolic form: verbal, logical, mathematical, symbolic form as the case may be. The process of doing this might be called symbolic transformation, a name used by the philosopher, Susanne Langer [12]. It is the process of going from more or less subjective "things in here" (pointing to one's head) which we feel, to some kind of symbolic representation. This may be written, spoken, sung, danced, built, painted, drawn, chiseled, or whatever. The representations of an effector in the simple ways I have shown are only a few of an essentially infinite number of symbolic transformations. But if we understand these few, then we can see how organized connections can be made between things outside of us, and feelings, and concepts, so that all take on enhanced meaning.

Proceeding further to the most general approach of

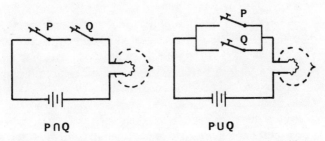

FIGURE 3.8 Embodiment of the relations "and" and "either, or both" in simple electrical circuits.

all, we enter the realms of philosophy. I shall show in principle the essential features of several points of view; for what we are trying to do here is to weave enough of the net of organized connections to show how meaning inheres in it, without trying to complete the entire pattern. To complete the pattern would be manifestly impossible: it is too complicated; it is too comprehensive; and it is in a state of flux at all times.

Our first aim will be to develop a scheme which places what we have already said in this chapter in context in the field of scientific epistemology. This scheme, which calls heavily upon the ideas of three scientist-philosophers—Max Planck, Henry Margenau, and F. S. C. Northrop—must be taken as a metaphor. I have later paraphrased the ideas of these philosophers quite freely, but the essence of the matter is given in the following quotation from Henry Margenau [13].

> Let us then acknowledge what is evident: An act of perception may be heavily weighted on the side of immediacy; I may dreamily or joyfully dwell among the ineffable, loosely integrated aspects of a clouded, sunlit sky. Or it may be pregnant with rational relations, as when I watch the swing of a galvanometer on a scale, expecting confirmation of a causal prediction. Again, a concept may be so abstract as to invite no response from the world of data, as for example the idea of a unitary matrix or a differential operator. Or it may be accented on the intuitive side, as the concept of a man or a tree. We believe

that experience can move continuously between all four of these, that there are *typically* rational and *typically* sensory parts of cognition, and that it is wrong to ascribe to mind, as the receptacle of experience, one special faculty of perception and another of reasoning. [NOTE: The term *perception,* when used without qualification, is intended to be synonymous with sensation, sensory awareness, and the like. It may designate the content of the perceptive act as well as the act itself, both being aspects of the same experience in the view we advocate.] Certainly, concepts and percepts can in general be distinguished, and we shall continue to regard them as discernible; but they merely form extreme types of activity, or results of activities integral to the process of knowledge.

Most of this activity is in the field of concepts; what is immediately given in sensation lies, figuratively, in a thin limiting layer, or on a limiting plane of experience. We are endowed with the ability to pass from there to any point among concepts, arbitrarily far from the limiting plane.

This relation between the analyzable components of experience and knowledge is diagrammed in Figure 3.9. The line "*P*" represents a section through a plane that extends indefinitely up and down, perpendicular to the paper. This represents the "thin limiting layer" upon which or close to which experiences are plotted. The plane suggests the analytically shallow nature of pure,

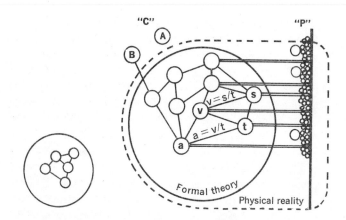

FIGURE 3.9 Redrawn, with permission, from Henry Margenau, *The Nature of Physical Reality: A Philosophy of Modern Physics* (McGraw-Hill Book Company, 1950), Figure 5-1, p. 85. "P" is the Plane of Perceptions: "C" is the Field of Constructs.

factual, immediate, aesthetic, imageful perception. On and close to this plane are plotted what Northrop calls concepts by intuition [14]. Here are found the "objects of physical science," the sources of the independently determined magnitudes upon which and through which the laws of natural science operate. The magnitudes, derived from these sources, are the numerical and non-numerical values that describe the properties of things—for example, that water at atmospheric pressure freezes at 273.15° Kelvin. They are independent because they represent the way things are: the inherent property of the things—in this case water—to behave this way.

To the left of the Plane of Perceptions are plotted, as small circles, what Northrop refers to as concepts by intellection. These are called "constructs" by Professor Margenau to emphasize that they are invented. For example, one might consider such constructs as displacement (s) and time (t). In physical science, as distinct from daily life, these have meanings that are specified in a certain invariable way by their definitions. For us, in daily life, time sometimes runs fast, sometimes drags interminably; and we may even say and feel that some experience "stops the clock." But constructed time, t, flows evenly on to the measured pace of a standard clock, or to the sequence of pulses of an atomic oscillation. Suppose you timed a race, or a physical experiment, by counting pulsebeats, as was done before the era of the clock. You can see, at once, the effect of excitement! Or take displacement, s. In physical science this is the distance between two points in a space delineated by some frame of reference. It represents a magnitude (a length) and a direction (angles to a fixed axis). But in our daily life displacements, for example, from breakfast table to classroom, may take us by meandering ways, and uphill or downgrade, through a "space" which is by no means homogeneous and isotropic—that is, the same in all directions. We do have frames of reference, such as streets, but our commonly sensed spaces are many: visual, tactile, olfactory; and they change with time, and for different persons. No wonder that Margenau can say of *constructed* space that it "towers above these others by virtue of a postulated uniformity which . . . both welcomes and in large measure defies the onslaughts of immediate experience."

The important point is that, as closely as can be determined, all physical scientists treat these constructs in the same way. They use them in what appears to be the same manner in practice, adhering closely to the defined meaning. Thus each can repeat the observations and manipulations, represented by the double-line pathways, from perceptions to constructs and, although starting from a quite personal perception, by following rules of operation, and applying the connoisseurship that he has learned from his teachers and his own work, arrive at the same construct. This is why the field of constructs "C" is named the public world of science. What the scientist may associate with these words from a sensual or other very personal, poetic point of view is another matter. But this would not be good *scientific* usage. These constructs are pretty naked of connotations. Their denotations are as strict and spare as possible—often stated in mathematical terms.

Constructs are usually capable of being defined verbally, and quantified mathematically, although of course I do not set these two modes of statement in opposition. Constructs, to be useful, must be connected to each other by at least two relations, indicated by the single lines; or by a single and a double line at least. For example, s may be connected to t to produce a construct "velocity" (v). This is speed in some specified direction. The definition of v, which shows the relation, is $v = \Delta s/\Delta t$; that is, displacement per unit of time: familiarly, speed in miles per hour. The deltas (Δ) are introduced to show that we are describing processes. That is, the velocity is the rate of change of s with respect to t. The symbol Δ means "a small change in". Velocity may also be connected to a derived construct "acceleration" (a) by the relation $a = \Delta v/\Delta t$: the rate of change of velocity with respect to time. Displacement, in the sense of a length, is connected to constructs such as area, and volume, and so forth. All of these are connected by operational recipes to perceptions. A construct such as A, which has no connections, is irrelevant; and a construct such as B, which has only one connection and hence leads nowhere, is useless. The former might be the construct "Snark" (which in this case has some connections to equally isolated concepts, such as "Boojum") [15]. It is irrelevant to physical theory. The latter, B, might be, to use Margenau's example, a color assigned to an electron —e.g., "pink." There is no way of substantiating this attribution. It does no harm, but leads to no new knowledge. The loop drawn about the set of multiply connected constructs represents the area of physical theory. The broken line represents physical reality.

For our purposes in this chapter, we need to notice that the physical theory is what may in general be named a "formal theory." This is a set of axioms, or postulates, which are connected by rules, or equations, and so forth, which do not violate logic. What converts the theory to experimental and technological usefulness is that it is connected to nature, as symbolized by the double lines. There are many formal theories, in mathematics, physics, and elsewhere, that have no known connections to nature. One is shown in Figure 3.9. They are interesting mental constructions, and remain speculative unless by some discovery they are connected to nature. The many single-line connections between constructs represent logical validation of them; the double lines represent empirical validation.

I have sketched these ideas for the purpose of drawing attention to, and illustrating, several points related to meaning. The diagram in Figure 3.9 relates specifically to the physical sciences. A somewhat different diagram must be drawn for the area of the humanities. This will be taken up in Chapter 6. We are interested, here, in the principle.

Given the deliverances of our senses, which we symbolize as being on, or near, the plane of perceptions: how do we get to the construct? We say that this step requires induction; that it involves a creative act. When, for example, Michael Faraday created, or invented, the construct "magnetic field," and devised experimental methods for demonstrating it, then afterwards anyone with the requisite equipment could verify for himself the construct, and connect it to his own observations with magnets. Thus passage leftward in Figure 3.9 symbolizes inductive, intuitive activity. This applies also to finding new connections between constructs, and to developing new constructs.

The reverse passage symbolizes deductive activity. One unpacks the conclusions, someone has said, that are already present in the premises, the constructs. One deduces the consequences that are expected to follow from the relations between particular constructs. If, in testing the deduction by experiment, he makes a hit on the plane of perception reasonably close to the predicted spot, then he has validated the constructs. Many philosophic questions find room to exist in the expression "reasonably close." The practical person finds quite adequate validation of Newton's laws of motion in seeing the astronaut bring his capsule down within a few miles of the waiting vessel. I feel sure that the astronaut himself is well satisfied. The question is moot in more subtle physical deductions. All involve creative acts.

From another point of view, one might classify the relations at the plane of perceptions as existential. The relations between constructs may then be classed as essential laws. The term essential, here, means that there is something ideal about them. They purport to be absolute: reality, nature, is relative *to them* in this view. Actually, these laws do not correlate with mundane phenomena in an absolutely exact way. The rules that link the constructs to the plane of perceptions have to allow for contingencies and, certainly at the atomic level, these correlations are statistical in nature. The plane of perceptions is the seat of contingency—of things that might have been otherwise. Moreover, and this is an important point which is discussed by Polanyi and Bohm, this is where the inexhaustibility of nature shows itself.

Earlier in this chapter we distinguished between the operational principles of a machine and the materials of which it is constructed. Figure 3.9 presents this distinction in diagrammatic form. The operational principles are found in the field of constructs. They are absolute in the sense that they would guarantee invariable success to a machine. But *the fact is* that they can be reduced to practice only through embodiment in tangible materials. This makes them liable to failure through the contingencies that are immanent in the nature of things. Thus there enter considerations which can be extended over the entire range of knowledge and experience, from the behavior of inanimate things to that of human beings. The range of meaning of these ideas is thus extended indefinitely.

The discussion of Figure 3.9 has been analytical in emphasis because it has had to be discursive: we could write only of one thing at a time. It is true that things of the intellect—that is, knowledge—are gathered into the field of constructs, and that things of perception and in general, experience, are placed close to the plane of perceptions. But none of them exists alone, except things like *A* and *B*, which essentially have no meaning. Each derives meaning, definition, and validation through its multiple connections with the rest, and through them to the whole. Everything hangs together; everything is related and comprises a whole. This is partly what I have tried to suggest in describing the formulation as that of a metaphor. But I also wish to retain for this metaphor the status of a *Gestalt:* of a picture of the whole to be grasped as a whole human activity.

We return, now, to a postulate advanced in the previous chapter, namely that when the Humanities, Sciences, Philosophies, and Technologies are brought together into a whole, functioning system, there emerge ethical imperatives which confirm and extend the noblest ideals that mankind has collected and treasured.

I pointed out that there are primitive cultures which, in the sense of having a coherent world view, could be called sacred—as distinct from secular. I shall now suggest that a secular culture is characterized by fragmentation; unrelieved specialization. Its organization cannot cope with its complexity, and it is moving toward or is actually in a process of, breakdown, such as Toynbee described in his study of Great Civilizations [16]. He described the tragic and helpless writhings of the spirit between abandon and self-control; truancy and martyrdom; the sense of drift and the sense of sin; the sense of promiscuity—vulgarity and barbarism in manners and art, *lingue franche,* Syncretism in religion; the sense of unity—not its reality; of archaism and futurism, in short, what he calls the Schism of the Soul. In this context certain of the dangers that face us today appear in a clear light, and I shall discuss these at some length in my final chapter.

From the scientific side we see that if our constructs

have an absolute character, to which reality is relative (see also Chapter 5), and if we forget the necessary connections to nature—where an inexhaustible supply of surprises awaits us—we may fall into a trap which I have already remarked. We may think that we have "the word" in some way. Uncultured persons may, indeed, fall most readily into this trap, and then be surprised at how soon they are drained; surprised at the sterility, loss of identity, loss of creativity that ensues.

Men of such diverse backgrounds and temperaments as Nicholas Berdyaev [17], David Bohm, Paul Horgan [18], and Michael Polanyi have called attention to this state of affairs. In the final chapter I shall spell out these matters further, and by that point I shall have suggested a program by which we may heal ourselves. To lay the ground for this endeavor has been the object of these early chapters. In the following chapter we shall see how the intellectual structure of the college and university, formulated in the metaphor of a sphere of knowledge and experience, expands the concept of meaning presented here.

I have tried to show how we make connections between perceptions, for example "things out there," and concepts, "things in here" (pointing to my head). I have shown in a truncated form how pattern-forming, naming, classifying activities connect for us verbal statements, geometric and mathematical statements. These connections will serve, for the present, as prototypes of symbolic transformation. They make it possible to grasp somewhat more easily the extraordinarily complicated, subtle, and comprehensive ideas presented in Figure 3.9. The essential point that I wish to leave clearly stated at the end of this chapter—in preparation for its extension in the following one—is that this figure implies the web of relations that has been found and constructed in this area of science. This is meant to *imply,* since we do not need to repeat, with the needed modifications, over and over again the formulations for other areas of science, the great strength, the sense of meaning that inheres in science. For if, as I have suggested, meaning inheres in organized connections, in relatedness, then surely we have in Figure 3.9 a metaphor of its embodiment.

NOTES

1 Abraham H. Maslow, *Toward a Psychology of Being* (D. Van Nostrand Co., Inc., Princeton, N.J., 1962), p. 15.

2 A. N. Whitehead, *The Aims of Education, and Other Essays*. A Mentor Book (The New American Library, New York, 1949), p. 26.

3 The quotation from Max Planck is from *The Universe in the Light of Modern Physics*. Translated by W. H. Johnston (W. W. Norton & Company, Inc., New York, 1931), p. 61.

4 "To be is to be related." I have not been able to recapture this quotation. The sense of it is to be found on pp. 28 ff. of A. N. Whitehead, *Science and the Modern World*. A Mentor Book (The New American Library, New York, 1952 [The Macmillan Company, New York, 1925]).

5 George Boole, quoted by Alice Mary Hilton in *Logic, Computing Machines, and Automation*. Meridian Books (World Publishing Company, Cleveland, Ohio, 1964), p. 163.

6 Roger J. Williams, *Free and Unequal* (University of Texas Press, Austin, Texas, 1953), pp. 109, 110. For further biochemical data, see his *Biochemical Individuality: The Basis for the Genetotropic Concept* (John Wiley & Sons, Inc., New

York, 1956). A summary statement, with implications, is to be found in his *You Are Extraordinary* (Random House, Inc., New York, 1967).

7 Pierre de Latil, *Thinking by Machine: A Study of Cybernetics* (Houghton Mifflin Company, Boston, Mass., 1957).

8 Michael Polanyi, *Personal Knowledge: Toward a Post-Critical Philosophy.* Harper Torchbooks (Harper & Row, Publishers, New York, 1964 [University of Chicago Press, Chicago, Ill., 1958]), pp. 328 ff.

9 David Bohm, *Causality and Chance in Modern Physics.* Harper Torchbooks (Harper & Row, Publishers, New York, 1961 [D. Van Nostrand Co., Inc., Princeton, N.J., 1957]).

10 W. Ross Ashby, *An Introduction to Cybernetics* (John Wiley & Sons, Inc., New York, 1958).

11 Venn's diagrams, logical relations and modern mathematics, are simply and authoritatively discussed by Irving Adler in *Thinking Machines, and The New Mathematics.* Signet Science Library Books (The New American Library, New York, 1961 and 1960, respectively).

12 Susanne K. Langer, *Philosophy in a New Key: A Study in the Symbolism of Reason, Rite, and Art.* A Mentor Book (The New American Library, New York, 1951 [Harvard University Press, Cambridge, Mass., 1942]).

13 Henry Margenau, *The Nature of Physical Reality: A Philosophy of Modern Physics* (McGraw-Hill Book Company, New York, 1950).

    The quotation from Margenau is from pp. 55 and 56.

    The short quotation on constructed space is from Margenau, p. 72.

14 F. S. C. Northrop, *The Logic of the Sciences and Humanities* (The Macmillan Company, New York, 1947). For extensions and illustrative use, see his later books: *The Complexity of Legal and Ethical Experience: Studies in the Method of Normative Subjects* (Little, Brown and Company, Boston, Mass., 1959); and *Philosophical Anthropology and Practical Politics* (The Macmillan Company, New York, 1960).

15 "Snark" and "Boojum" are from Lewis Carroll, "The Hunting of the Snark," in Roger Lancelyn Green, Editor, *The Book of Nonsense* (E. P. Dutton & Co., Inc., New York, 1956), pp. 3 ff.

16 Arnold J. Toynbee, *A Study of History. Abridgment of Volumes I to VI,* by D. C. Somervell (Oxford University Press, New York, 1947), Chap. 19.

17 Nicholas Berdyaev, *The End of Our Time,* together with an essay on *The General Line of Soviet Philosophy* (Sheed & Ward, New York, 1933).

18 Paul Horgan, "The Abdication of the Artist," in *Proceedings of the American Philosophical Society, 109:*267 (1965).

4

The Sphere of Knowledge, Experience, and Action

In this chapter I extend the web of meaning, partly knitted in the previous chapter, to cover the entire intellectual content of the college or university (and by implication also the elementary schools). My objectives, here, are to show a way of describing the intellectual structure of the college (and from this point, when I use the word college I mean also university) so that unity is emphasized; to give a means of encouraging the student to find meaning in his work; to suggest—but only by implication, since this is not a primary objective—how the college catalog and course offerings might be revised; to give enlarged meaning to the academic enterprise. First I shall construct a metaphor, discussed at some length elsewhere [1], and then I shall use it to further the objectives enumerated above.

We begin with a definition of the Sciences and the Humanities. I open a college catalog, and find the course offerings alphabetically listed by departments. Gathering these together into groups according to subject, I arrange them in the logical order shown in Figure 4.1. Physical Sciences, for example, comprise Physics, Chemistry, Astronomy, Geology. Physical Biology, Biophysics, Molecular Biology would lie between Physical Sciences and Biological Sciences, which latter comprise Botany and Zoology. Ecology clearly extends over a range from Physical Sciences to and through Biological. There is space, then, for a large number of disciplines to be plotted in this figure. I define the right-hand semicircle of disciplines as the Sciences, and the left-hand as the Humanities.

This diagram is given the meaning I want it to express by certain restrictions and explicit statements of what is meant. It is not meant that Literary Criticism is in some way "opposite" or opposed to Biological Sciences; or that there is some "opposition" between Mathematics and History or Political Science. What is meant is that there is a logical relationship, symbolized by the circular line, between all these groups of disciplines. The disciplines are all different: they are given different names. Their practitioners often inhabit different premises; and each group has its own budget (that is, they are real!). But they are related. Thus on the right, moving from Physical Sciences to History, one finds increasing preoccupation with single entities. Where in Physics

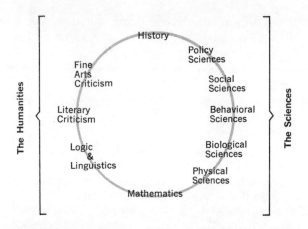

FIGURE 4.1   Definition of The Sciences and The Humanities.

and Chemistry one is usually concerned with swarms of identical particles, in Political Science and History one must usually become involved with, and study, the single, determinative individual. The logical arrangement on the left is not as clear, but perhaps it might be suggested that here a concern with discursive modes of communication shades into that with presentational modes, a distinction made much of by the philosopher, Susanne Langer [2]. In any event there does seem to be a logic in this arrangement, and if it is not neat and precise, this is because the phenomena that are ordered here are not neat and precisely delineated.

Another point: the relationship is what counts, not

the orientation of the whole figure, for this may freely be rotated provided that the logical relation is not disturbed. I say this to counter the kind of semantical maladjustment that might recognize a slight at seeing Mathematics in the "inferior" position "at the bottom." I have had this criticism leveled at the diagram. The answer, given by Professor Joel Hildebrand, is "Of course! It's *fundamental!*"

This diagram shows, explicitly, the important relationship of Mathematics and History as bridging disciplines: each is both a science and a humanities subject. The somewhat scientific aspects of History have been the burden of many essays, and I would side with those essayists who do not take an either/or position, but admit, implicitly if not explicitly, the fact that History as it is usually taught comprises aspects of both the Humanities and the Sciences. I shall support this statement below. Mathematics, a highly theoretical subject, yet partakes also of humanistic and scientific aspects. One objective support for this statement comes from the fact that a college may offer the choice of either a B.A. or a B.S. to the graduating Mathematics major. This kind of evidence must be weighed against the facts that some colleges give only A.B. degrees while still others offer the option of B.A. or B.S. degrees throughout the Sciences; and still others offer a B.S. in, for example, Literature, as does Purdue. Nevertheless, I take it as significant that a catalog of Rice University [3] described Mathematics thus: "As one of the most modern of sciences and, at the same time, one of the most ancient of the humanities, mathematics is regarded as an integral part of any general education." We must recognize with pleasure that there are these bridging disciplines that help to support the unity of the Sciences and the Humanities in the larger synthesis implied in Figure 4.1.

To carry the image somewhat further, we might consider whether this circle might be given coordinates. Without pressing the matter too far we might distinguish, between the Humanities semicircle and the Sciences, certain differences in *emphasis* in the means of communication utilized most commonly by their practitioners. In the Humanities, difficult matters are communicated through analogy, and when really most difficult, through metaphor. On the Science side, the drive is toward the use of ratio. I shall return to these distinctions below.

Looking from the top of the circle toward the bottom, one can discern another range of emphases: at the bottom, the content of the discipline is most abstract and formal; at the top, most embodied and concrete. Thus we might give to each discipline-cluster in the circle a pair of rough coordinates. In Fine Arts Criticism, for example, persons tend to be less abstract, more concrete, and more personal in their use of metaphor and analogy as means of communication. In Political Science, while one is concerned with the concrete—the individual and the crowd—the attempt is made to formulate relationships in analogies and ratios. Mathematics tends to be the most highly abstract of the disciplines, the one in which analogy and ratio are invoked to formulate relationships.

The Sciences and the Humanities are of course different, and our assignment of them to opposite semicircles implies this, and implies some oppositeness. However, this oppositeness is not to be construed as opposition; rather, the explicit intention is to imply that each supplements the other, as the right eye supplements the left for greater depth of vision and a more just view of the world.

To make places for all the disciplines that do not appear in Figure 4.1—Law, Medicine, Religion, Philosophy, and all the engineering subjects—we need to develop a more comprehensive figure. This requires previous discussion of the activities that are carried out in the college: the activities that support study, teaching, and research in the *whole* field of knowledge, experience, and action.

To deal thoroughly with this matter, we have to analyze activities and present the results of the analysis in discursive language. This is unfortunate, in a sense, because the activity generally should be grasped as a whole. However, we have no other course, and as a remedy I present Figure 4.2. This shows the three types of activity, each shading into the other, and all forming a whole: data gathering, synthesis, and application to practice.

Data gathering is an activity that includes observing, recording, reporting, collecting of data. I have set it off from synthesis because I want to call attention to how difficult it is to be, for example, a reporter and

KNOWLEDGE, EXPERIENCE, AND ACTION

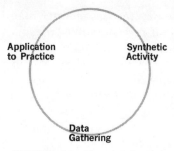

Application to Practice

Synthetic Activity

Data Gathering

FIGURE 4.2 The Intellectual Activities.

nothing else. Just to write down, or speak, or otherwise record what one experiences, is most difficult. The temptation to editorialize is great. Patterns of one kind or another, relationships and predictions, tend to intrude. One need simply ask a group of students to write down only what they see when shown a simple demonstration to find out how many are unable at first to do solely this. Indeed, in the world of practical affairs pure reporting seems to be decreasing as an activity, and news stories and other releases are dressed up with editorializing: perhaps obscuring what actual facts there are.

It would seem to be the case that man is a pattern-forming animal. This is why a pure list of observations may seem offensive. One wants to make sense of it, to find some pattern—that is, to organize it. The physicist, Dr. John Bowman, late of the Mellon Institute, once told of an experience he had had in the early days of computers. He was invited to "match pennies" with a computer by calling "heads" or "tails" while the computer at the same instant made a call. It turned out that after a certain number of calls (I seem to have the number 60 associated with this story) the computer practically always won. One of his hearers was greatly depressed by this: "You mean that the computer was smarter than you?" The explanation was that the computer "remembered," the way a cash register "remembers" prices punched into it preparatory to totaling them, all his calls, while he did not memorize or record those of himself or the computer. It then searched the list with high speed for each call and, finding a pattern, used it, following the program built into it, to predict his next call, and to use this information to beat him. Thus the computer was giving evidence that his brain worked in a patterned way. This kind of objective evidence is quite comforting. Suppose that our brains worked in purely random or chance ways? There would be no learning; no need for education; no culture. Indeed, the only way to break even with the computer was to flip a coin and *call what appeared; heads or tails*. The computer then was forced by its program to operate with a random series of numbers, and a stalemate was reached. But a human being cannot, out of his own mind, extract a sequence of random calls.

Thus the inevitable step that accompanies data gathering is synthesis: the finding of pattern; the classification of the data; "this is more like this one than like that one." Synthesis leads, as was implicitly described in the previous chapter, to the development of constructs; to the construction of hypotheses that may lead to theories and to laws. In sum, the activity of synthesis is the activity whereby meaning is developed and enhanced by finding and explicitly showing the relationships between data, *whatever* the data may be. Nowhere

KNOWLEDGE, EXPERIENCE, AND ACTION

is this shown better, as a human characteristic, than in studies of comparative religion. *Everything* that occurs in the Heavens and on the Earth is fitted into an organized pattern.

There is perhaps no intellectual activity more delightful than finding relationships; than manipulating symbols and concepts; than building theories; and inventing hypotheses and laws. This activity can, at the same time, lead very far astray if it is pursued to the exclusion of the third activity: application to practice. In order to be genuinely certified as operationally valid, theories should go through and survive the ordeal of application to practice. Nature, the way things are—this is the final arbiter. The rare cases are those divorced completely from immediate influence upon human affairs. A purely formal theory in mathematics is an example of a theory that cannot be reduced to practice in the sense described, yet may be certified as formally true, or correct. This is a pure invention based on axioms that have no connection to experience (Figure 3.9), yet are logically and completely internally connected. Such a theory may later become empirically validated, as in the famous case of Riemann's geometry which, at first a pure mental construction, was later used by Einstein and Minkowski to describe outer space, and thus given empirical reference.

Of course I am speaking here of fairly abstract matters. Physics, Chemistry, Biology, Psychology, Sociology, Political Science, all, as academic disciplines, require this validation of theory. And so do the academic humanistic disciplines. One cannot imagine much credence given by serious scholars to a theory of the modern drama if it has not been based on a good deal of data (existing, modern plays) and has not been tested against new plays that were written or discovered after the theory had been laid down.

At the same time such criteria do not seem to be applied in some fields of action in relatively short-term, concrete as well as abstract, matters. One need only think of mass movements and "the true believer" to agree with Eric Hoffer. In a discussion of what makes a doctrine effective, he says [4]:

> It is obvious, therefore, that in order to be effective a doctrine must not be understood, but has to be believed in. We can be absolutely certain only about things we do not understand. A doctrine understood is shorn of its strength. Once we understand a thing, it is as if it had originated in us. And, clearly, those who are asked to renounce the self and sacrifice it cannot see eternal certitude in anything which originates in that self. The fact that they understand a thing fully impairs its validity and certitude in their eyes. . . . If a doctrine is not unintelligible, it has to be vague; and if neither unintelligible nor vague, it has to be unverifiable. . . .

Thus the analysis we have made is not applicable to mass movements, or to activities that partake of these characteristics. It is in this sense partial. (And we do restrict it to the college scene.) One can, of course, raise the question whether a great mass movement, based on a vague or unintelligible, or unverifiable doctrine or ideology does not by its very success validate the doctrine. I believe that in the long run the only final arbiter is the way nature behaves, man being included in nature, here. One marked difference between the tests of validity of movements of this kind and practically all scientific tests of validity is that usually the scientific tests yield an answer within a short time: minutes, hours, or days. Very seldom does one have to wait more than a year or so. But ethical truths, and spiritual truths, usually require a lifetime—perhaps even centuries—for their validation [5]. This means that we must call upon the deliverances of history in such long-range validation procedures. The impact of Teilhard de Chardin's *Phenomenon of Man* is, I think, due to his skillful use of both history and natural science to test his hypothesis [6]. I shall return to this matter of testing against the way that nature is, in the final chapter.

We now take the last step in constructing our metaphor of the Sphere of Knowledge and Experience (Figure 4.3). We place the ring in Figure 4.1 as an equatorial belt about a sphere, and we now conceive of the Sciences and the Humanities as *hemispheres*, rather than as the semicircles of Figure 4.1. These shade off toward the top of the figure into Philosophies, and toward the bottom into Technologies. Both of these terms are plural, although one is, of course, at liberty to imagine an ultimate at

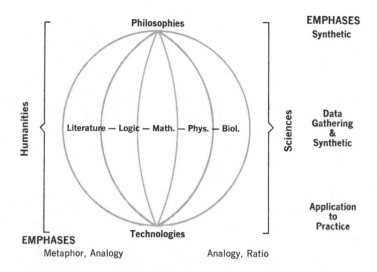

FIGURE 4.3   The Sphere of Knowledge, Experience, and Action.

any point on the sphere. On the right is placed a vertical axis labeled "Emphases." This is an attempt to show that among different groups of disciplines, stress is laid upon different activities described in connection with Figure 4.2. For example, in the pure Sciences and Humanities disciplines of the equatorial belt, chief stress is laid upon data gathering and synthesis. In a Chemistry course one has to learn a great deal of data: properties of substances, and so on; as well as theoretical explanations of the behaviors of these substances. As an example, one investigates the theories of the formation and the breaking of bonds between atoms as one substance reacts with another. In Literary Criticism one has to accumulate a great deal of data in connection with his studies of theories of style; of adequacy; of high seriousness. But in none of these pure disciplines can application to practice be ignored. The Chemist has his laboratory, or his chemical literature, against which to test theory. The Literary Critic, too, must apply his theory to practice in order to validate it. However, and this is my main point here, the *emphasis* is on data gathering and synthesis. Indeed, the pure Scientist and Humanist sometimes tends to disparage the work of the applied man, thus clinching my point in an all too anthropoid way.

The Philosophies tend to emphasize synthesis, in so far as they deserve the name *Scientia Scientiarum*. But here, again, the other activities must be practiced, for purely synthetic activity can be stultifying. There is nothing like an internally completely self-consistent theory to lead one astray. We have seen examples of this in theories that remain self-consistent only by excluding or ignoring contrary fact. If we insist that application to practice is important in validating a philosophy, we must also be prepared to find that there are many valid philosophies. For no single one that is attainable is able to comprehend all legitimate points of view. And, further, nature is inexhaustible, and full of surprises. We are permitted, of course, to extrapolate to such a universally valid Philosophy as an Absolute.

But only if we have a great deal of data *and* a theory to guide the extrapolation.

The disciplines on the lower half of the sphere in Figure 4.3 require some discussion because of a prevalent state of confusion with respect to the nature of technology. The Technologies are those disciplines wherein the *emphasis* is on application to practice. The figure clearly shows what we find to hold, namely that there are Humanistic as well as Scientific Technologies. The confusion that we mentioned above is twofold: only Sciences are thought of as having technological sides, that is, engineering; and, equally wrong, that which is technological is thought of as being science.

The Technologies belong in the college because although emphasis is on application, the other two activities are carried on concomitantly and in relation to application to practice. If application were all, then one would have a trade school. This is not to derogate the trade school, but to distinguish it from the college or university. In the college or university the technology disciplines include a study of the technology. That is to say, reflection upon the methods, activities of data gathering, and synthesis. There is study of the method of the methods, so to speak; the development of heuristic. This certifies that the stature of these disciplines is the equal of those in the other two regions of the sphere.

The very oldest disciplines were technologically based. They grew out of the uses of life. Rashdall has pointed out that originally the university was a scholastic guild, of masters or students [7]. There were theoretical studies as well as practical ones included in the grammar, rhetoric, and dialectic studied in the very earliest of these associations. The earliest American universities were technologically oriented, with their accent on preparing young men for the practice of Law, Medicine, Politics, and Religion. This orientation was accentuated in the land-grant colleges. The supercilious attitude that some of our colleagues take toward technologists, while at the same time some of them derive income from industrial consultation, has all the trappings of ignorance and intellectual arrogance—two of the more flagrant sins in academia.

The great old disciplines of Law, Medicine, Politics, and Religion were Humanistic Technologies. Consider, as an example, Law. To practice Law is to apply to the exigencies of *this* particular case the theoretical disciplines of jurisprudence. In many cases the lawyer brings to bear, in the case at issue, results, precedents, theories from a wide range of disciplines, including literature, drama, and the social and natural sciences. This is diagnostic of a technology: that it focuses into practice a range of theoretical disciplines.

As another example, take Medicine. This is the only one, of these ancient Technologies, that has any fixed undergraduate prerequisites beyond a good, general education. The physician, the humanistic, scientific technologist, brings to bear on *this* one sick person, a range of Sciences as well as of Humanities. For he learns about the human heart in his anatomy lessons and his courses in pathology. But often the cure must come through that knowledge of the human "heart" found only in literature, drama, and the other Fine Arts. Here again, the particular case is the focus of a range of theory.

This is surely, too, the case with the practice of Religion, wherein the science and art of Theology, with associated disciplines, literature, psychology, sociology, are brought to bear on the problems of *this* congregation, or of *this* soul.

So we must recognize that there are Humanistic as well as Scientific Technologies. Advertising, the fifth estate, much of propaganda, are Humanistic Technologies. And many departments of engineering are changing their names to "applied science," for example, "applied physics."

We may remark, further, that differentiation between the regions of the sphere on the basis of these emphases can be correlated with our discussion of Figure 3.9. The Philosophies may be conceived as being *chiefly* occupied with the field of constructs and the relationships therein, particularly those farthest from "P"; the Pure Sciences with the leftward movement from data to constructs, and with the relationships between constructs. The Technologies are mostly concerned with the movement rightward, from theory to the Plane of Perceptions, with particular emphasis at this Plane.

As with Figure 4.1, the important implications in Figure 4.3 are the relationships. The figure may be rotated in any direction to bring any discipline to the "top" but the relationships must be preserved. There is space on the figure for any subject whatsoever that may be taught as an intellectual discipline in the college. For example, some courses in Philosophy may lie close to the equator near a group of Sciences, or close to Mathematics. Some courses in Literature or Fine Arts may verge toward the technological side. Some may occupy a wide area of the surface, others a very narrow area. We do not attempt to show *quantity* of knowledge and experience, nor the passage of time. For this one would need a sphere that bulged out here, collapsed there, and so on. This Sphere of Knowledge, Experience, and Action is to be taken as a metaphor. It serves as an intellectual scaffold to aid comprehension by the student of the unity of knowledge, experience, and application, and to enable him and his teacher to place any subject in context in the academic sphere.

As an illustration of the use of this scaffold we may place on it the classical questions. Near the top of the sphere, as it stands in the figure, one might place the question, "What can we know?" Along the equatorial belt lie the disciplines whose function in part is to answer the question, "What do we know?" And below these, the question, "What can we do?" finds its provisional answers in the Technologies.

Another axial gradient of *emphases* may be placed

horizontally below the sphere. This has to do with methods of communication. The ideal in the Sciences, reached in a few instances in Physical Science, is to state knowledge in the form of the mathematical ratio. Such great ratios as $F = G \, m_1 m_2 / s^2$ for the Law of Gravitation, $F = C \, q_1 q_2 / s^2$ for Coulomb's Law, $F = ma$, and $E = mc^2$ exemplify peak attainments of this effort. Most experimental results, however, are comprehended only through imperfect ratios: verbal or mathematical analogies. These have special uses—the uses of imperfection. They suggest hypotheses, and the sites of imperfection—the cracks in the analogies, one might say —serve as loci for the introduction of experiments. Thus is most research done.

In the Humanities area there is little recourse to mathematical ratio, although there are some applications now appearing in the area of Linguistics—as in stylometric analysis. Chiefly, reliance is placed upon analogy: models. But there are those communications that require more powerful tools than these. There are the ineffable thoughts and feelings and experiences which we need somehow to make communicable. In the history of mankind there have been men who have found ways to speak, paint, compose, or otherwise communicate what was previously incommunicable. They have done this by means of the most powerful tool for such uses: metaphor. "The metaphor," says Ortega [8], "is perhaps one of man's most fruitful potentialities. Its efficacy verges on magic, and it seems a tool for creation which God

forgot inside one of His creatures when He made him."
Metaphor, myth, analogy, and models on the one side,
emphasized more in the Humanities, range over to
analogy, models, and ratio on the Science side. But
scientists, too, use metaphor when other means fail.
Similarly, one might make the case that, relatively
speaking, comparing one group of disciplines with the
others, the emphases are on emotion in the Humanities,
cognition in the Sciences, action in the Technologies—
but of course, *never exclusive emphasis.*

This diagram is neat, and idealized. But it refers to
things that are far from neat; that are confused, with
loose ends. The pattern is discernible, and this is what
is shown. My objective here has been to expand the
meanings, partially disclosed in the previous chapter, to
include the whole Sphere of Knowledge, Experience,
and Action that is available in the college. If this is
grasped, then the beauty of an Alma Mater as a whole
functioning body can be sensed. The student and teacher
need no longer feel alone, and alienated, and unrelated:
they can see themselves as part of a great and noble
tradition.

NOTES

1 The subject of this chapter is discussed at greater length and more completely in Harold G. Cassidy, *The Sciences and the Arts: A New Alliance* (Harper & Row, Publishers, New York, 1962).

2 Susanne K. Langer, *Philosophy in a New Key: A Study in the Symbolism of Reason, Rite, and Art.* A Mentor Book (The New American Library, New York, 1951 [Harvard University Press, Cambridge, Mass., 1942]).

3 The quotation from the Rice University Catalog is from the 1952 edition, p. 133. [I am indebted for this reference to Dr. Isaac Dvoretzky.]

4 The quotation from Eric Hoffer is from *The True Believer: Thoughts on the Nature of Mass Movements* (Harper & Row, Publishers, New York, 1951). Cf. pp. 79–80.

5 On the remark about the validation of ethical and spiritual truths, see Charles Allen Dinsmore, *Religious Certitude in an Age of Science.* The McNair Lectures, 1922 (University of North Carolina Press, Chapel Hill, N.C., 1924).

6 Pierre Teilhard de Chardin, *The Phenomenon of Man.* Harper Torchbooks (Harper & Row, Publishers, New York, 1961 [Harper & Brothers, New York, 1959]).

7 Hastings Rashdall, *Universities of Europe in the Middle Ages*. Edited by F. M. Powicke and A. B. Emden (Vol. I: Oxford University Press, London, 1936).

8 The quotation from José Ortega y Gasset is from *The Dehumanization of Art: And Notes on the Novel*. Translated by Helene Weyl (Princeton University Press, Princeton, N.J., 1948), p. 33.

5

The Well-Tempered Liberal Sciences

Since the beginning of this century the Sciences, always undergoing changes, have been changing even more radically, and now these changes are reflecting themselves noticeably in the behaviors of scientists. For this reason I have undertaken in the first part of this chapter to describe some of the effects of these changes as they may influence the role of science in the liberal education of our young men and women in college.

By "Sciences" in the title of this chapter I mean the activities of scientists, and the knowledge that they accumulate; and by "Scientists" I mean specifically those natural, behavioral, social, and policy scientists who study, primarily, phenomena in non-man-made nature, and who study the natural, non-man-made aspects of human beings. By "Liberal Sciences" I mean to invoke the modern sciences that are emerging from the constraints of nineteenth-century materialism, positivism, and related dogma, and which retain an openness to change while at the same time holding on to proven values. By "Well-tempered" I mean something broader than liberal in the above sense; I mean adjusted to the exigencies of liberal education. I mean that the claims made by the Humanities, by the Philosophies, and by the Technologies are fitted to those of the Sciences; that the Sciences adjust to a role in the sphere of knowledge and experience as cooperating and not autonomous disciplines. The well-tempered liberal sciences would therefore be expected to contribute to clarifying, and perhaps to giving a tentative answer to, some of the crucial problems raised by humanists, philosophers, technologists, thus giving added meaning to the whole.

In this chapter and the following ones, I continue to deal with subjects in which I am no expert. I remain sensible of this fact. But it seems to me that not to attempt to penetrate the barriers of language, of experience, of sensibility, between disciplines is to connive with fragmenting forces. This is to be against life. For it is an old wisdom that inaction inevitably leads to decay; that effort against the fragmenting force of neglect in any area is an important kind of behavior and, to put it in reverse terms, that in the long run "we don't get anything for nothing." I shall have to speak about matters concerning which I cannot qualify as an expert, and I shall be sustained by the knowledge that *outside of our own specialities all of us are laymen:* that if barriers are to be crossed it is inevitable that most of them be crossed by laymen.

In its Galilean beginnings the movement that later came to be known as The Scientific Revolution was no appeal to reason. "On the contrary," says Whitehead [1], "it was through and through an anti-intellectualist movement. It was the return to the contemplation of brute fact; and it was based on a recoil from the inflexible rationality of medieval thought. . . ." The revolution that was set off by this revolt has developed in breadth and depth for twelve generations and has brought such vast changes in our ways of thinking that it is difficult for us even to realize them. Indeed, to be able to approximate the thinking of those days requires special historical training, and only with this training might it be possible to grasp how different our intellectual milieu is from that of three hundred and fifty years ago.

As happens with successful revolutions, what is new and revolutionary at one time becomes the Constituted Authority of the later day, and breeds its own opposition. And there has been growing in the last hundred years a new anti-intellectualist revolt. It invokes the brute facts of feeling, to put it baldly, against the inflexibly rational mechanisms of positivistic science and the cold, harsh inevitability of physical law. This movement, identified with Kierkegaard, in the first place, has brought new insight and has recalled forgotten ideas. These it has brought to bear upon opinions and philosophical judgments that have been based upon a science which already, by the end of the nineteenth century, was showing signs of scientific inadequacy. This movement has gained in strength, even as the older science has been replaced.

When in the early days of the scientific revolution the findings of Copernicus, Kepler, Galileo, and many others, showed us that we are inhabitants of a relatively small planet that spins lonely in a great void, with no near neighbors save Luna, the then prevalent "Ptolemaic" assumption that man and his Earth were at the center of the physical universe received a blow from which it has not recovered. This change in view came to be known as the Copernican Revolution. It was against the consequences drawn from these scientific revelations, and from those drawn from the Newtonian, and later the Darwinian revelations about the Heavens and the Earth, and the creatures upon the Earth, that the revolt I have referred to was directed.

But something very drastic happened in physical science at the beginning of the twentieth century. Out of the discoveries which eventually led to Einstein's Special Theory of Relativity, published in 1905, and the state of scientific work which confirmed and interpreted the great theory, and the later General Theory, has grown another scientific revolution. This was christened by Bertrand Russell a long time ago, it seems to us now, as a "Ptolemaic counter-revolution" [2]. The theme, suggested by this name, was caught in 1929 by Archibald MacLeish in his poem "Einstein" [3]:

> . . . He lies upon his bed
> Exerting on Arcturus and the moon
> Forces proportional inversely to
> The squares of their remoteness and conceives
> The universe. . . .

The newly conceived universe is not the old one with a new façade. A conceptual mutation has occurred. For in this new universe man has been brought back into the center again, but not in a physical sense. The Spanish philosopher, Ortega, put it this way [4]: "In the physics of Einstein our knowledge is absolute; it is reality that is relative." We have touched on this in previous chapters.

But action and reaction continue to express themselves, and a readjustment in our thoughts is beginning to manifest itself. This has been given impetus particularly by the scientist-philosopher, Michael Polanyi, in rich and eloquent books; but it rests, as do all such movements, on earlier insights and intimations. It acknowledges the truths that have been disclosed by Gestalt psychology, Phenomenology, Relativity, and Quantum Theory and, relentlessly following the paths illuminated by these new concept-clusters, arrives back at an enlarged concept— a concept of scientific objectivity which Polanyi finds exemplified by the Copernican theory. Polanyi says [5]:

Objectivity does not demand that we estimate man's significance in the universe by the minute size of his body, by the brevity of his past history or his probable future career. It does not require that we see ourselves as a mere grain of sand in a million Saharas. It inspires us, on the contrary, with the hope of overcoming the appalling disabilities of our bodily existence, even to the point of conceiving a rational idea of the universe which can authoritatively speak for itself. It is not a counsel of self-effacement, but the very reverse—a call to the Pygmalion in the mind of man.

This is not, however, what we are taught today. To say that the discovery of objective truth in science consists in the apprehension of a rationality which commands our respect and arouses our contemplative admiration; that such discovery, while using the experience of our senses as clues, transcends this experience by embracing the vision of a reality beyond the impressions of our senses, a vision which speaks for itself in guiding us to an ever deeper understanding of reality—such an account of scientific procedure would generally be shrugged aside as outdated Platonism: a piece of mystery-mongering unworthy of an enlightened age. Yet it is precisely on this conception of objectivity that I wish to insist in this introductory chapter. I want to recall how scientific theory came to be reduced in the modern mind to the rank of a convenient contrivance, a device for recording events and computing their future course, and I wish to suggest then that twentieth-century physics, and Einstein's discovery of relativity in particular, which are usually regarded as the fruits and illustrations of this positivistic conception of science, demonstrate on the contrary the power of science to make contact with reality in nature by recognizing what is rational in nature.

The echoes of earlier work, selected, corrected, amplified, and creatively supplemented by Polanyi, include the recognition that we participate in the existence of that which we comprehend. This is something the humanist can understand. We develop theory to mediate in the way I have symbolized in Figure 3.9. Between the things that are immediately accessible to our senses at the P plane and reality, we develop the web of meaning shown here in special terms for physical science. And out of the deliverances of our senses and our minds arises the recognition of "what is rational in nature." It is this kind of knowing that is actually practiced by scientists; it has made its provisional peace with doubt *and* faith as heuristic principles; with the hazards of potential error and consequent falsification; with the requirements of beauty and profundity that are placed by our minds upon that which we would regard as true. In his Preface [5] Polanyi makes a statement which can stand as a definition of what should be conveyed to the student by the well-tempered liberal sciences:

The power of science to grow by the originality of individual thought is thus established within a cosmic perspective of steadily emergent meaning. Science, conceived as understanding nature, seamlessly joins with the humanities, bent on the understanding of man and human greatness. Man's ideals, unfolding in action, come into view.

Formal symbolization of this seamless union is to be found in Figures 4.1 and 4.3.

I mean, then, by the liberal sciences, all those sciences which have grown up in the clarifying light of relativity theory, quantum theory, Gestalt theory, and phenomenology. It is interesting, and important, that this scientific revolution is turning the direction of the revolt which I described above away from the initial existential extremes. It has abandoned many of the presuppositions against which that revolt was directed. *For this reason it becomes more and more possible for fair-minded people to meet in those great areas of knowledge and experience where the Humanities and the Sciences supplement each other.*

In examining the role of the liberal sciences in education we have to deal with at least two aspects of education: there is the function of the educational process to impart factual knowledge and encourage the student to gain certain experiences; and there is the function of continuing the student along the road toward becoming a better person. These endeavors, or functions, involve the interaction of student and teacher mediated, perhaps, through the subject of study.

We know a good deal about methods for the inculcation of knowledge, and in general we know ways of examining how the process is coming along. For knowledge is true statements about facts of various kinds, and, provided we understand the pitfalls that beset the search for the kind of truth called knowledge, we do have hopes that we can teach better and better in this aspect of the educational process.

I am not sure that we can teach experience: we can provide sources of experience and encourage the student to use some and consider the importance of others; and we can show the student results of the experiences of others so that he may gain understanding directly as well as vicariously, in other words, through laboratory participation, demonstration, and reading. There is an old saying that the teacher opens doors; the student must choose to walk through.

These, knowledge, experience, and action, help the student toward the goal of becoming a better person. This part of his education also depends on his life with other students and on the personal precepts and evidences of his teachers. These last two aspects, the gaining of experience and the progress toward becoming a better person, are difficult to judge, yet they are aspects that need most attention today, it seems to me, as I listen to my students. The Sciences are, as we saw (Figure 4.3), one of four educational areas. By educational I mean suitable as mediators between teacher and student in the educational process. The others are the Humanities, the Technologies, and the Philosophies. The four are sufficiently different from each other that they must be distinguished, if we are to avoid common mistakes and confusions. The distinctions were made quite clear in the previous chapter. One matter needs to be emphasized, and that is that none of the subjects in these four areas can be comprehended by a list of courses. It is obviously necessary to have an outline for a particular science course and a schedule of subjects for a program, but these by themselves do not constitute science, or even *a* science. The reason is that the Sciences and the other educational disciplines are as much tools as they are ways of using them. We have to think in dynamic, in process, terms. Educationally employed, as I have said, science and any of the other three involve the interaction of student, teacher, and subject. A great deal of the success in teaching rests upon the development in the student of that connoisseurship (Polanyi's term), that skillful knowing and skillful experiencing that can lead to skillful achievements, theoretical and practical, which serve to make him a better person; affirmatively to unfold him.

The expression "well-tempered" in the title of this chapter is taken from music. The strings on the piano are not tuned to the exact mathematical ratio that a rigid equation would require. Instead, each is adjusted a little to the needs of the others so as to enhance the harmony of the whole, *as heard by the human ear*. So, with the well-tempered sciences, each is not treated as an autonomous discipline, but is adjusted to the needs of other sciences and to those of the Humanities, for the more harmonious functioning of that nourishing mother, Alma Mater.

What I mean, here, needs to be spelled out somewhat, because departmental autonomy is one of the most jealously guarded principles of academia. I do not, by any means, suggest a violation of the taboos that protect departmental autonomy in respect of budgets and staff appointments. What I do urge is that the *discipline,* the conceptual structure of the subject, not be taken as a thing unto itself (a common situation in the graduate school, where one or a small cluster of related disciplines demand utter allegiance of the neophytes). If a discipline—say Chemistry—is treated in the sense I inveigh against, it becomes isolated and loses meaning to the student. Of course, the presumptive professional major may be persuaded of eventual pie in the sky, there to be eaten after he has successfully undergone the ritual trials that tradition decrees for his own good; but the nonscience major is too often repelled. To be sure, a skillful teacher can show the power, beauty, elegance, and subtlety intrinsic in a subject so as to occupy the full attention of the student. But how much added effect would come from explicitly making of this subject a paradigm of every science, thus giving this power, beauty, and subtlety the widest reference. This way of teaching a subject is part of what I ask for when I speak of treating the discipline in a well-tempered way.

But there is more to it than this. The subject can be

taught in the light of the *whole* curriculum (Figures 3.9 and 4.3). The student can be encouraged to *discriminate* between ways of approach to problems; to think about the uses of cognition and emotion as checks and balances on each other and as guides to action. I would see, here, a means of showing the importance of making distinctions, as also of finding similarities; of teaching a generous skepticism and an intelligent openness to new insights. All this, let me say, can be done in teaching any scientific subject. It is particularly effective at the elementary levels in college. The point is that the well-tempered, liberal approach implies that the subject is part of a whole; that though the college offers him three or four hundred courses of which he can take only twenty in his four years, yet through these twenty the student finds access to any of the others: access that he can avail himself of in later years. And let me add that the well-tempered approach does not need to decrease in any appreciable way the quantity of substantive material the student is required to know. If some small amount of material has to be dropped in order to gain a little time, there are usually to be found enough trivia that can be sacrificed. It is, essentially, a matter of *style*. The subject is taught in the presence of the whole curriculum: the last few minutes of a class period may be taken to open minds a little wider; perhaps to glance in another direction; to support and reward intelligent behavior.

Let me emphasize, lest the intent of what I have

said be misunderstood, that I believe a great many science teachers follow these precepts. I know of some. And I am not under the illusion that what I am describing is new, or very radical. As I wrote in the Preface, I am concerned to rally these teachers against an insidious creeping professionalism which, pushing specialization ever further down into the undergraduate levels, can in the long run only fragment, divide, and weaken our culture. To teach in the well-tempered, liberal style is not easy, yet our free life may hang upon it.

What we offer to the student, in addition to the needed substantive material of the particular subject, in the style of teaching I have described, is the understanding of the processes of perception and conception, and the connections between them, together with the implications for the student's own life. These connections have been sketched in Chapter 3, where from the verbal realm we progressed via the algebra of classes to embodiment in hardware. When a chain of meaning of this kind is traced, and I offer this only as an illustration of what I mean, for other teachers will find ways of doing this that are more congenial to them, as perhaps from a biological, or sociological, or other point of view, the student experiences an exciting lift. All of a sudden he sees the wide panorama of knowledge and experience laid out before him, *and accessible.* But perhaps the most important discovery he can make is that although there are many paths that might be followed, the following of one tells something about the landscape that might be viewed from another. The approaches of Chapters 3 and 4, when combined, provide a corrective to the attitude expressed by one of my students:

> It is difficult to convince a student that the material he is studying is relevant either to his own life or to the world around him. This, perhaps, is the prime killer of budding scientific interest: a feeling of irrelevancy. Balls rolling down inclined planes, electrons shooting out of the nucleus of atoms, molecules flitting faster and faster as the heat and pressure increase—it is difficult, I suspect, for anyone to completely avoid the sensation that these things are rigged.

This is one kind of attitude, and I see it in the behavior of students in physics and chemistry demonstrations. This is entertainment, they seem to say. It is not intellectual food. Every teacher who has had this experience and has tried to devise an antidote, knows how difficult it is to achieve one. I have offered one possible prescription in the previous remarks, and a second possible prescription follows.

But let me add the comments of another student. I asked him what in his opinion was the direction in which science courses should move. He said, "In the direction of philosophy," and continued:

> I stress philosophy [in the liberal sciences] because this *word* represents the most intense field of interest

among freshmen. I say *word* because those men who enroll in philosophy courses in hopes of having some of their questions about the world and life explored, are disappointed to find themselves being driven through a wasteland of semantic jungle-gyms which seem just as irrelevant as their other courses. To make of science a relative to abstract thought would provide them with a constantly stimulating view of the world around them, a world in which technical progress represents not merely the accumulation of new information, but new and radical implications for life as a whole.

This man would not object to doing a great deal of substantive work in science—he was willingly memorizing large numbers of words, and connecting rules, fine distinctions in meaning, and so on, in his language courses—if only he could see its relevance to life; to *his* life especially.

So I come to the second, and related, way in which a science course could help the student become a better person. This is, to help him interpret his culture. I have suggested, broadly, how science is affecting our culture. I have suggested how a comprehensive view of knowledge and experience might be intuited. But the whole realm of the Sciences is so vast, and the rolling journals pile up waves of data so threateningly high, that it is not surprising to find the student, and teacher, for that matter, discouraged. How do we meet this state of affairs?

In Chapter 3 I referred briefly to cybernetics. We

now return to this subject as an introduction to a state of optimism, and to the final topic of this chapter. We are concerned with what the individual can do in the face of the inundation of data.

In the first place it must be suggested that very likely the term "knowledge explosion" is a misnomer. Knowledge has increased, certainly; information in the sense of data has exploded. One asks, to underline the distinction, just how many *new, general* principles have emerged out of this "knowledge explosion"; and the answer is that there have not been many. The student, teacher, or investigator is clearly faced with too much data: too much *for him*. I do not mean to imply that there should be a cessation of work. Such a suggestion would be nonsensical. Most persons enjoy carrying out an investigation; a paper reporting an elegant method, a new measurement, a discovered relation, is a source of pride. It is worth while in itself, even if it advances no great new knowledge. Further, the large portion of this work is closely related to economic consequences, whether in science, technology, or in the matter of promotions, with its attendant benefits, or whatever. So there is no sense in proposing a moratorium on data production. The problem lies elsewhere. But first, the question of the role of the person himself.

We return to the problem raised in Chapter 3, that of organizing particulars into coherent wholes, with concomitant expansion of meaning. We pick up the thread at that point.

KNOWLEDGE, EXPERIENCE, AND ACTION

Cybernetics was defined by its inventor, Norbert Wiener, as the science of control and communication in the animal and the machine [6]. Another definition, which speaks better to our present condition, was given by Louis Couffignal: cybernetics is the art of assuring the efficacy of an action [7]. For our purposes, we will examine the organization of an effector of a high degree: an effector that employs feedback.

I spoke, in Chapter 3, of a system as a set of variables. This is a difficult concept for some persons. What is meant is that if one is concerned with a material object such as a household heating system, let us say, an oil hot-air heating system, with oil-burner firebox, ducts for heated air and return ducts, electrical power conduits, oil supply, associated thermostat, and the entire household, one can describe it in terms of the hardware. But this description is good only for systems of this kind; perhaps even only for this particular installation. Instead, then, one talks about the *behavior* of the system: the changes in temperature; the amount of oil consumed in a given time; the volume of air processed through the furnace; and so on. And then one takes the final step: he generalizes still further, away even from words like temperature, air, furnace, so that only *relations* are of concern. We have seen a prototype of this approach in the discussion in Chapter 3 where we started with classes of things, and progressed to algebraic expressions which had no explicit reference to material objects; also in the discussion of Figure 3.9, where it was shown that

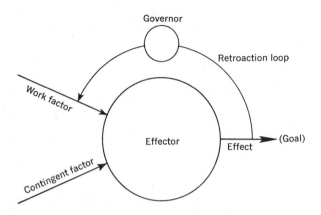

FIGURE 5.1   A simple effector with feedback.

imageless constructs (*C* field) were inductively generated from concrete imageful perceptions and other experiences. These constructs could be manipulated according to the rules of logic and mathematics, and then from the results of such manipulations, consequences could be deduced that would return us to the *P* plane. This is in essence the approach we take here. Of course, it is often helpful to visualize a system in some concrete terms.

The system, in general, is open to its surroundings. For example, the heating system must *receive* oil, or other fuel, and electricity for power and control. It affects its surroundings by throwing off heat, smoke, and other fumes. We say, then, that the surroundings influence the effector through its input, and the effector influences the surroundings through its output. There is always this openness about a system. Moreover, we must remember that one of the inputs must be labeled "contingent." Here things which might not have occurred, such as accidents, reach the effector. The effector can be diagrammed, using a figure from de Latil [8] (see Figure 5.1). The effect is the heat produced; the work factors are the electricity and oil. Contingent factors are such occurrences as a sudden cold spell, or a door left open to the outside of the house. Effectors of this degree rely on feedback. A small amount of the effect is utilized to carry information to a governor, or detector-governor, about the state of the output. The governor has been designed and set, or "programmed," to give a response desired by someone, who has thus set the goal of the effector. For example, the thermostatic detector-governor has been set for 68° to 70° by indicator dials. Then when the temperature of the house falls below 68°, the detector reacts to this change, activates the governor, which turns on the burner. Additional, simple effectors are connected to pump the oil, turn on the blower, and turn it off on a designated cycle. When the temperature of the room in which the thermostat is placed reaches 70° the detector-governor turns off the burner, but the blower continues to operate as long as the firebox remains hot. Thus, in this simple system we have an effector which, through the operation of the retroaction loop, maintains the temperature of the room, and the house, within set

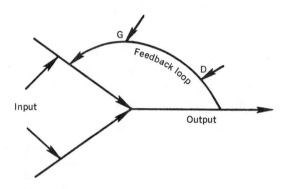

FIGURE 5.2 A simple system with feedback.

limits and against ordinary contingencies. The system cannot overcome absence of fuel, or loss of power, or excessive cold. But within the programmed limits it does a good job. This serves as an example of an effector with feedback. We diagram it as shown in Figure 5.2. It is to be noticed that a machine such as the household heating system is made up of many submachines. There is a motor to run a pump which forces oil into the combustion chamber, and a switch to turn on this motor; another motor, with blower and switch, to distribute the warmed air; there is the thermostat detector-governor switch. These are all lower-degree effectors, and each lacks feedback. They are *organized* into the complex machine. The efficacy of the action of the machine is a function of this organization.

We have barely touched on what is a subtle and in its higher reaches an extremely complicated subject. One further development in these concepts will provide enough background for our uses here.

It is apparent that systems of tremendous complexity may be diagrammed in this way. Thus the behavior of a human being might be so diagrammed. At this point, the "system" has become a metaphor (in my view); however, this does not destroy its usefulness. I believe, that is, that at the level of living beings, and particularly human beings, we are not at present justified in applying the tenet of reductionism: that we can reduce the system to a set of simple, "atomistic," primitive effectors whose organization alone is sufficient to ensure the emergence of the properties of the total system. I believe that we must explicitly leave the conceptual door open for the entry of, for example, hitherto quite unsuspected factors. Proponents of reductionism may claim that this approach is necessary as a generator of hypotheses that lead to experiment. I see no necessity here that cannot be met by a more open, tentative position; by one that admits of the lessons taught by history: that nature is inexhaustible; that we have barely begun to expose the mysteries of the universe; in other words, by the position I take here.

With this caveat, suppose then that we consider the system shown in Figure 5.3:

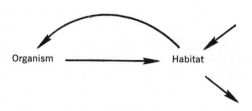

FIGURE 5.3   Linked effectors.

This links together two effectors. The organism might be a student; the habitat at one particular time might be the classroom; at another, his lodgings plus roommate; in another context one might think of him in interaction with the institution, as I did in Chapter 2. An essential feature of this diagram is that it shows *explicitly* that the organism influences, and is influenced by, the habitat, and that the system is open to its environment (which might be thought of as the habitat of the system-as-a-whole). Also it makes clear that there is input to (arrows going into) and output from (arrows going out of) the system-as-a-whole. The concept is familiar to ecologists, who traditionally think in terms of wholes.

Now let us make this a little more explicit by means of Figure 5.4.

114

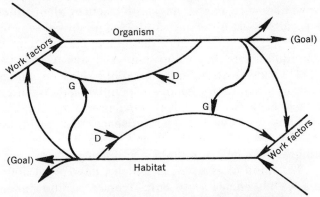

FIGURE 5.4 Coupled systems of organism-habitat.

Part of the output of each subsystem is fed back to its own work-factor(s) through detector(s) (*D*) and governor(s) (*G*); and part of the rest affects the other subsystem; and the remainder is output to the environment.

Let us take a specific example, the student-institution system-as-a-whole. And let us look at it broadly in its intellectual aspect (as distinct, say, from its athletic, social, economic, parietal, and so forth, aspects). The goal of the institution is to start the student well on his way to an education that will continue even after he leaves the institutional interaction. The goal of the student, let us say, is the same. It will usually be more restricted and personal, while that of the institution might be described *sub specie aeternitatis,* one would hope. In this aspect of the interaction the student's output comes in the form of essays, term papers, experimental reports, class attendance, conferences with teachers, all of which, *as variables*, are quite normally given quantitative evaluation. The student's output, these data, are fed into the institution where they are examined, analyzed, and evaluated. The evaluation, in the form of grades, encouragement or admonitions, honors or punitive actions, and so on, fed back to the student, influences his output. At the same time his behavior influences the institution; while its own evaluation of itself, through the detectors and governor, help it to hold a firm course.

This kind of analysis, of which I have given only a bare sketch, comes as an enlightenment to the student. He suddenly sees himself as connected to the institution by bonds that are in process of development, and by variables to some extent under his control. Moreover, by analysis of his own situation and of the structure of the college (the institution) he can identify the governing functions and so, if he will define his goal, he becomes capable of action. Many students who merely drift through college, and there are untold numbers of these, might thus be induced to take an active part in the control of their education.

But the most important implication of an analysis of this kind is that a small part of the effect, of the output, is sufficient if applied to the governor in the proper way, to swing the entire effector; and to influence the output; and hence to determine its efficacy of action. Thus the individual *can* have an effect, even in a mass society, if

116   KNOWLEDGE, EXPERIENCE, AND ACTION

he knows what he wants; understands the way the system is organized, which means that he has identified the *operative* detectors and governors, not just the titled ones; and is willing to apply himself at the appropriate times, to the appropriate people or things. The student can take control of his education as a responsible person, if he sees these connections. He himself gains thereby in meaning and centrality. He is enabled to interpret his culture through the unifying power of the cybernetic approach.

Finally, I turn to the tremendous central problem of the well-tempered liberal sciences: the question of course-content where pressure from the professionally oriented instincts of many department-faculties operate against both the liberal and the well-tempered needs of the student. I say department-faculties because often the individual faculty members are, by and large, quite reasonable people—they, too, live in the world, and recognize the needs of breadth. But get them together into a committee, or a whole faculty of a department, and the lowest common denominator seems to take over. They look upon every student as a potential recruit to their profession, which by implication is clearly superior to every other, even though a clear look at the statistics would show them that if their department were to be chosen by more than, let us say, 5 per cent of a given class, they could not handle the numbers; and that this danger has never threatened, since they have never had more than 2.5 per cent of the class elect to major in their field. These numbers are not quite taken out of my hat. I use them to illustrate the important point that the professional proselyters are often quite unrealistic and dog-in-the-mangerish to their own loss and that of the student.

Moreover, many department-faculties feel that since they have worked hard to devise the best preprofessional program for their majors, it should certainly be good enough for everyone else to take.

We all have, I am sure, seen these attitudes at work, if we are associated with a college [9]. The only antidote that I have found is to get such a committee to believe and to adopt the basic premise that not all students are potential science majors. We do not have to argue whether they *should* be. The corollary of this is that since this is so, the course given to them need not fulfill preprofessional prerequisites, and there is the further supposition that literacy in science is an asset to the Humanities major.

We then come to the content of the actual course. I have discussed this in connection with one particular course elsewhere. I would like at this point to emphasize that a great many dedicated teachers are exploring this question at the present time. That this is so is in the record, and some of the results of their explorations have been published. I do not wish to review these approaches. Instead, I shall conclude with certain general principles which seem to me valid and which bear on course content. Let me say, immediately, that I assume that a well-tempered, liberal course may be given in any science department, and that undoubtedly some courses of this kind are now, and always have been, given. I here offer encouragement.

We would like such a course to enable the student to continue on with more science courses. Thus it should not be terminal in intent. It should not be a survey course because such courses cannot avoid being superficial, and cannot avoid insulting the intelligence of the student. It should be given by one teacher unless all who cooperate in giving it attend all the lectures and consciously fit their individual contributions into a coherent whole. Otherwise the assumption is that the students will integrate the diverse presentations, an assumption which may imply that they are more intelligent than the teachers.

Whatever the subject, then, the course should have substantive content. To decide on the content, the teacher should, in my opinion, try to stand aside, temporarily at least, from the tribal customs of his department. He should ask himself, as objectively as possible, what he believes will still be important in his subject twenty years from now, and what in his opinion will be affecting the lives of young people as they grow older during this period. This is obviously a difficult and risky judgment to make. It is clearly much safer to give a survey which is sure to hit at least some of the important matters, even though giving them only a lick and a promise. But it would be far better to choose carefully a very few key topics, and to treat these *in depth,* with great care to build the background needed for a clear understanding of them, ruthlessly omitting irrelevancies, no matter how picturesque. The main point is to provide well-understood factual material, as a basis.

The student should be involved with this material: he should be drawn in by the teacher, using all the devices the teacher can command. These might include exercises, both qualitative and quantitative, term papers, laboratory exercises, or projects. Sometimes a reading period can be used for a long laboratory project, perhaps carried out under a professor in another department, perhaps one the student may be considering for a possible major.

The problem with many laboratory experiences, suggested by the student I have quoted, is that they seem irrelevant to the student. One way of dealing with this is to begin with epistemology, and to get the student deeply involved, conceptually and experimentally, with problems of knowing. This approach is discussed by Mrs. Abercrombie, and I recommend her book most highly [10]. It comes as a great awakening to most students to realize how biased and fallible they can be. But I would also emphasize that the purpose of such experiences is not to destroy the student but to raise questions and to guide the student to *replace* that which he rejects with what is to him more satisfactory. I shall revert to this in a similar connection in the following chapter: one should never take away from the student more than one returns.

As I said before, my purpose is not to prescribe

course content, but to advance principles. The course syllabus is merely a tool in the hands of the teacher. There is only one general principle for ensuring good courses that I can devise from my observations: obtain the best possible teachers, and then trust *them*.

NOTES

1 A. N. Whitehead, *Science and the Modern World,* Lowell Lectures, 1925. A Mentor Book (The New American Library, New York, 1952 [The Macmillan Company, New York, 1925]), p. 9.

2 Bertrand Russell, *Human Knowledge: Its Scope and Limits* (Simon & Schuster, Inc., New York, 1948), p. xi.

3 Archibald MacLeish, "Einstein," in *Collected Poems of Archibald MacLeish* (Houghton Mifflin Company, Boston, Mass., 1926), p. 43; see also p. 50.

4 José Ortega y Gasset, *The Modern Theme.* Translated by James Cleugh (W. W. Norton & Company, Inc., New York, 1933). See p. 138 and pp. 135 ff.

5 Michael Polanyi, *Personal Knowledge: Towards a Post-Critical Philosophy.* Harper Torchbooks (Harper & Row, Publishers, New York, 1964 [University of Chicago Press, Chicago, Ill., 1958, 1962]). The longer quotation is from pp. 5, 6; the shorter is from p. xi.

6 Norbert Wiener, *Cybernetics: Or Control and Communication in The Animal and The Machine* (Technology Press, John Wiley & Sons, Inc., New York, 1948). The central third of this book is mathematical; the rest is accessible to the layman.

KNOWLEDGE, EXPERIENCE, AND ACTION

7 Louis Couffignal is quoted on p. 15 of Gordon Pask, *An Approach to Cybernetics*. Science Today Series (Harper & Row, Publishers, New York, 1961).

8 Pierre de Latil, *Thinking by Machine: A Study of Cybernetics*. Translated by Y. M. Golla (Houghton Mifflin Company, Boston, Mass., 1957). This book is nonmathematical and full of insight. It is written with flair.

Three other books on cybernetics may be recommended: Neville Moray, *Cybernetics*. Vol. 131 of *The Twentieth Century Encyclopedia of Catholicism* (Hawthorne Books, Inc., New York, 1963). This is a sound and completely nonmathematical introduction.

W. Ross Ashby, *An Introduction to Cybernetics* (John Wiley & Sons, Inc., New York, 1958). This book is rigorous and mathematical in its approach; however, it is accessible to a person who has had high school algebra. It is excellently written, and the author has provided exercises, with answers, to help the reader test himself.

Alice Mary Hilton, *Logic, Computing Machines, and Automation*. Meridian Books (World Publishing Company, Cleveland, Ohio, 1964). A comprehensive treatment of the subjects in the title, and thus an introduction to aspects of cybernetics.

The definition of habitat and environment

was formulated in this way by E. F. Haskell, *Ecology, 21*:1 (1940).

9 The application to the college is taken from Edward F. Haskell and Harold G. Cassidy, "General Systems Theory and Education: On the Unification of Science." A paper given at the 132nd AAAS Meeting, Section L3, Society for General Systems Research, Berkeley, California, Dec. 30, 1965. And Harold G. Cassidy, "Wholeness: The University's Task," in *The Graduate Journal,* 5:160 (1962).

As an example of the kind of behavior that can be departmentally sanctioned, I know of the following situation. It was decided to offer non-science freshmen a combined course in Physics and Chemistry. These two departments were asked to cooperate in this course. They decided that each would offer one term, taught by the instructor, in his department. One of the instructors wrote a term-long course especially for the purpose. The other either did not have the time to write a suitable course or else could not bring himself to omit material from his regular, excellent full-year course. He tried to cram far too much material into one term. The resulting monster lasted three years, as I recall. The two half-courses, one in Physics and one in Chemistry, were taught by separate instructors who did not attempt to tie the subjects together. This implied that any integration would be done by the students; and further implied that the students were thus expected to be more concerned than the instructors. The students were explicitly insulted by the fact, perhaps done to make the classes smaller, that the very large number of students who first elected the course were assorted into two large groups, one of which took Physics the first term, followed by Chemistry, and the other Chemistry first, followed by Physics. Public notice was thereby given of the irrelevancy of the one course to the other, and to the denial of reason. Many students refused to elect the courses after the first year or so, and the Physics instructor, who had designed a thoughtful one-term course, expanded it into a highly successful Physical Science course. The reader may draw his own moral from this tale. It all happened many years ago, about twenty, and was highly discouraging to the young instructors who saw this unthinking operation carried out by their seniors.

Explorations of science courses explicitly designed for nonscience majors are now being carried out by several groups: the Commission on College Physics; the Commission on Undergraduate Education in the Biological Sciences; and the Advisory Council on College Chemistry, are some. Many teachers are also privately working in this area, I am sure. An excellent example of the good work being done can be found in the *Proceedings of the Boulder Conference on Physics for Non-Science Majors,* edited by Malcolm Correll and Arnold A. Strassonburg, for the Commission on College Physics (Edwards Brothers, Inc., Ann Arbor, Mich., 1965).

For discussions of courses, see the three papers published in the *Journal of Chemical Education,* 46:64 ff. (1969), by H. G. Cassidy, C. Keilin, and E. A. Wood, and the keynote address by William Kieffer, published in that journal, 45:550 (1968).

10 M. L. J. Abercrombie, *The Anatomy of Judgment: An Investigation into the Processes of Perception and Reasoning* (Basic Books, Inc., Publishers, New York, 1960).

6

The Well-Tempered
Liberal Humanities

In the introduction to their translation of the text of
Goethe's *Italian Journey*, W. H. Auden and Elizabeth
Mayer say of Goethe [1]:

> He always refused to separate the beautiful from
> the necessary, for he was convinced that one cannot
> really appreciate the beauty of anything without
> understanding what made it possible and how it
> came into being. To Goethe, a man who looks at a
> beautiful cloud without knowing, or wishing to know,
> any meteorology, at a landscape without knowing
> any geology, at a plant without studying its struc-
> ture and way of growth, at the human body without
> studying anatomy, is imprisoning himself in that
> aesthetic subjectivity which he deplored as the be-
> setting sin of the writers of his time.

Here, it seems to me, we have a clear statement of what the well-tempered liberal Humanities should foster, if they are in this day to be made relevant to the student's life.

"What made it possible and how it came into being." This phrase suggests an approach to understanding many difficult questions. A philosopher may ask, "What is beauty?" "What is truth?" Questions of this type are essentially unanswerable: they can only be discussed. The historian, or the critic, would ask, "What made it possible, and how did it come into being?" This question offers a starting point and a procedure, whether onto-genetic in nature, concerning itself with the history or development of the person or particular work, or phylo-genetic and concerned with the history or development of the species. This approach, impartially humanistic or scientific in its use of the emotions and intellect, may lead to clarification of the vague philosophic question, and to concepts of standards of beauty, truth, good, against which to try the particular work. Its chief virtue, perhaps, is the recognition of the role of processes, of the unfolding interplay of dynamic tensions that charac-terize life; it escapes from the dead end of a static, pre-sumed absolute. It is in tune with a powerfully flowing stream of modern thought.

The threads that weave the web of connectedness which unites the Humanities into a whole are the many-hued aspects of persons, their behaviors, dreams, thoughts—whether displayed through word, or deed, or artifact; in literature; music, sculpture, painting, and the other Fine Arts, or in the critical estimates of these; and in biography.

I say *persons*, intending to emphasize a distinction made, for example, by Martin Green, between persons and individuals, or entities. A person is unique; as an individual he is a member of a group and displays the characteristic or characteristics that define the group. As we saw, the person's uniqueness may be certified through exhaustive classification. Moreover there is scientific evidence for his uniqueness (Figure 3.2). One might enquire why such evidence is thought necessary when everyone knows the verdict. The reply points to the scientist's need of quantitative data. He feels more secure, with reproducible measurements in hand. To the humanist, the force of conviction generated through his methods may be so completely persuasive that confirmation by measurement is essentially irrelevant. Both approaches have their uses and, almost without saying, either may serve to support, or correct, the other.

The person is unique in the sense that he may choose when and how to react. It is a matter of freedom—of his autonomy, says Green—that is emphasized here. This person is the subject of literature and the arts, and is their object. But this does not imply sole preoccupation with the unique. (Some modern movements in the Humanities have gone far in this direction. For example, a concert may be performed once, and only once, because it is controlled in its progress by chance occurrences and is not recorded—perhaps wisely.) Indeed, most critical effort involves the attempt to weigh the work, whatever it may be that is being examined, against some standard; to test the unique thing against some distillation of great uniqueness. This does not mean that the highest-level abstractions may not require the most concrete embodiment in order to be communicated.

In their educational use at the undergraduate level, the liberal Humanities, concerned primarily and essentially with the person, with his soul, his psyche, his mind, his behavior, should be particularly directed to finding regions where the student is open to receive new conceptions. This is not because there is virtue in novelty, or change, but because if the possibility of modifying his interior life is there, then he can be helped to become a better, more sensitive, balanced, cultured person.

Here, as in the Sciences, I recommend opposition to present graduate school trends. The object of the liberal Humanities is not primarily to turn out scholars in the professional school sense. Some students will gravitate in this direction on their own inner urging, and must be encouraged. But the aim is toward something larger. Or perhaps I should say, wider.

For the Humanities to be well-tempered means, analogously to the requirement of the Sciences, that there must be a relaxation from ascetic specialization in the interest of the student who must live in this world pushed by science and technology. I have found an attitude among some humanists, of which the statement by one of them: "I've never had a course in science and I'm proud of it," is partly diagnostic. There seems to be real antagonism; that, and in some cases a withdrawal into the past; not, however, a withdrawal likely to bear fruit. For example, one young man with whom I was thrown was studying a Latin dramatist. He was going to become an expert on this man's works, he said, and will have read all of them. There exists a finite possibility since the work is presumably all known, and the language is dead, for this student to draw a nice neat line around a field in which he will know "everything." I asked, for it was my business as a teacher to ask, whether he had studied any anthropology: "No"; any sociology: "No"; any psychology: "No". Then what could he bring as *his* offering to the work? Footnotes upon footnotes, perhaps, but surely few new insights. This same type of myopia is far from unknown in the Sciences, of course, where one can become even more unbelievably narrow. And this man was still an undergraduate. I could visualize him, twenty years from now, guarding his niche like a prairie dog its own burrow; as sensitive, defensive, insecure, deeply ignorant, and uncultured, as his counterpart in science.

I suppose that pathognomonic of a certain segment of the Humanities is the Snow-Leavis embranglement. Leavis's reaction to Snow's *Two Cultures,* shrill, jagged, even vulgar, would seem to indicate a state of insecurity and withdrawal; "an alienation from the essential conditions of modern society," says Martin Green [2], and he continues,

> How could it be otherwise, when what is modern and challenging and painful about the present and future is so intimately associated with science, while the humanities deal so much with the past?

Green has given full credit to the contributions of Leavis, which he knows at first hand, and which he values, but he has also taken care to sound some of the depths of Science—to the extent of seeking out and taking college courses in mathematics, physics, and biochemistry. What I do wish to notice in the affair is the same sense of touchiness and uncertainty and withdrawal that I have found in many Humanities teachers. Green then continues:

> We shall need our full humanity, as Leavis says, to meet the sharp challenges of the future. But full humanity cannot be guaranteed by a literary sensibility so sharply distinct from and distrustful of other kinds of intellectual and practical experience.

The major scandal in college education today is that, with the exception of a few schools like Rensselaer Polytechnic Institute, the Humanities major leaves college having had only one or two courses in Natural Science, and an equally small number in Social Science. This state of affairs almost guarantees the continuation of cultural illiteracy in the majority of our population.

It is a form of national suicide for which must be held responsible the teachers in the Humanities *and* in the Sciences, as well as administrative officers.

The scandal seems to penetrate other depths also. Not only is the young man majoring in a Humanities discipline very likely to be illiterate in Science, and so unaware of the vast potential of inspiration for him that resides in the exciting, fundamental, earth-shaking discoveries in Science; he does not even think of himself as a Humanist. It is as though he has seen too many of his elders hiding in some overinhabited specialty, picking over the footnotes of what someone said about someone else's saying, or looking over their shoulders to copy some superficial (usually largely analytical) aspect of successful Science. The Humanist's noble birthright seems lost. He does not identify himself by any easy choice with what seems to him in too large a part sterile, or highly derivative. These impressions I get as I listen to the young students and teachers I encounter in the course of my teaching. I must not be misunderstood here. The same kind of footnote-worrying goes on in Science, and may discourage a student who sees it alone. However, there is so much that is new and relevant staring him in the face and challenging him in most Sciences that he seldom has much time to brood about the sterilities.

Sometimes one receives the impression that these young men do not realize how different is the Humanist's problem from that of the Scientist. The problem of the

Humanist, broadly speaking, is this, as I see it. Both Humanists and Scientists are concerned with ultimate problems (that is, how the World is), but the Scientist, by and large, is very choosy about the kind of problem he will attack. In principle all his problems are capable of solution or of something that satisfies him as a solution. Of course these problems are restricted, not in possible scope but in type: they are such as are amenable to his tools; to his conceptual tools and to the machines and apparatus that are the material embodiments of his concepts. *Everything else is left for the Humanist!* This is why the Humanist should never try to be a Scientist. His is a heavy burden of responsibility. This burden has two aspects: one is to balance and moderate the scientific, technological emphasis on artifacts; on the great machines such as computers; the great constructs such as genetic mechanism; the other is to rediscover, and redesign and innovate, so that what he says about men and women is relevant to present problems and responsive to present needs. While teaching our heritage, he interprets it in the modern idiom (Chapter 8).

Take the first aspect. Consider the plight of the scientist or engineer who designs a computer. He tells us that it is very like a moron; it is very fast, but has to be told exactly what to do. It has a limited vocabulary, he says, like pidgin English. The subtlety of concepts that can be dealt with in pidgin English is surely limited. (Professor Robert Singleton speaks analogously of pidgin Fortran.) But at the same time he has no other way of talking about what it does except in a language of familiar terms that by their common anthropomorphic reference makes us think of the machine as a giant "brain" that is bigger and therefore better than ours; that it has an infallible "memory," the small size of which, compared in quantity and subtlety, is mislaid in the compression of exponents; that it has an ability to solve problems, and therefore to "think," with unimaginable speed, although somewhere in the verbiage there may be lost the fact that the ability to solve these problems was inserted by the human programmer, and the types of problems do not include those where judgment is involved, or where intuition, imagination, *non sequiturs,* and irrational hunches play a role in an innovative solution. Popularizers with a low threshold of responsibility grab these words and make out of them a nightmare of claptrap for the fearful and uninformed.

The half-educated Humanist may easily fall victim to this dehumanizing twaddle. If it should be that his knowledge of history and the behavior of human beings in the face of striking inventions and discoveries reins in his credulity, alas—he is usually not equipped to rebut, deride, or otherwise provide an antidote for this stuff. The well-tempered Humanities would develop stouthearted Humanists inside and outside of colleges, who are critical and knowledgeable; who can seek out informed scientific opinion and understand it; and thus be able to maintain a balance on that front where scientific technology impinges on the public mind; where the results issue in action. For people—the great body of the public—will read poetry and novels; will attend plays and the movies; but they will not read scientific publications. Sometimes one has the impression that these media reflect with single vision the analytic image of how some things are in their ugly state. Might not one hope for two-way mirrors which would also suggest some measure of a man's possibilities? It seems to me that here the most vital and perhaps revitalizing hopes are appearing in the theatre. Scientists, too, need to be shown these visions. And what I have said, using the computer as example, is applicable to all the fantastic new tools or concepts that bear upon us: problems of genetic control, of conception control, of environmental pollution, of communications pollution, and so on. Scientists and scientific technologists need well-tempered Humanists and humanistic technologists to balance them; to keep the vision of a human being clear and central: at the controlling center of the modern kaleidoscope of artifacts.

As a scientist I would have been more hesitant in my strictures were it not for the eminent Humanists who have voiced the same or related concerns. For example, Paul Horgan, in "The Abdication of the Artist" [3], has said, in part:

> Some recent artists have abdicated their creative powers to the force of accident. Because much of life may seem idiotically random or chanceful in character, they have thought to find in random idiocies and the perversity of chance a true analogy for life at large.

Others were moved by the charm and sweetness —and perhaps the occasional terror—expressed in the art of primitive peoples to become primitives through sophistication—a procedure fatuous on the face of it, rather like the ecstasy of the tourist going native.

And Katherine Anne Porter in "A Country and Some People I Love" [4], says:

> We are being sluiced at present with a plague of filth in words and acts, almost unbelievable abominations, a love of foulness for its own sake, with not a trace of wit or low comedy to clear the fetid air. There is a crowd with headquarters in New York that is gulping down the wretched stuff spilled by William Burroughs and Norman Mailer and Ellison —the sort of revolting upchuck that makes the old- or Paris-days Henry Miller's work look like plain, rather tepid, but clean and well-boiled tripe. There is a stylish sort of mob promoting these writers, a clique apparently determined to have an Establishment such as their colleagues run in London. It's perfect nonsense, but it can be sinister nonsense too.

Also, in judicial vein, and making a point which is the root of my concern here—the poets and novelists, and practitioners of the fine arts may be corrupting the minds of our young people in a kind of antihumanism ("literature must destroy itself," "music must be silence, so that the only noise you hear is in your own head—a solipsistic ditty"). Rebecca West, in "A Grave and Reverend Book" [5], which reviews Truman Capote's *In Cold Blood,* says:

It is within the knowledge of all of us that life is often hard to bear. But it has oddly happened that our society which is, if not perfect, at least more generally comfortable than any society has succeeded in being before, has produced a literature quite often taking as its basis the pretense that life is absolutely unbearable. This pretense is behind some good plays and novels and some bad ones. A work of art does not have to be completely valid either in its facts or in its philosophy, so it may share the quality of imperfection with books and plays which cannot be classed as works of art at all. This pretense that life is unbearable is not accepted as literally true by any but a minute number of readers or writers; very few people commit suicide. But it is widely adopted as an intellectual counter, not an opinion which one sincerely holds and would act upon, but which one uses as a substitute for opinion when talking or writing, like the chips one uses when gambling at casinos. It then passes into general currency, in films, on television, in chatter, and so it happens that one day a naïve person with stronger dramatic instincts than most, and less sense of self-preservation, comes to believe that sophisticated people believe life to be unbearable, and therefore it is not terrible to carry the belief to its logical conclusion and to deprive his fellow men of their lives. . . .

KNOWLEDGE, EXPERIENCE, AND ACTION

What air do these people breathe not permeated with the culture we have made? Where else could they have caught this infection but from us? There is a hateful continuity between the world of literature and the world of Mr. Capote's criminals. . . . Literature must go its own way, sometimes a blessing to its age, sometimes a curse; for no soothsayer can ever predict when it is going to be the one or the other. All the same there are occasions when it is comprehensible why Plato felt fear lest the poets corrupt the minds of the people. But at any rate nothing but blessing can flow from Mr. Capote's book.

I have given these three quotations to suggest that my own comments, from outside, are not without validity. After listening to serious discussions of some modern literature—in this case, the novel and the drama—one gets the impression that in them, and in the minds of serious critics, "reality" is equated exclusively with the violent and the debased. In one such discussion there was, in some two and one-half hours of talk, not one single reference to nobility, to transcendence of self or culture; no application of the criteria that humanistic critics used to apply to the writing of earlier ages— writing which dealt with the same kinds of human behavior but with a sense of what a man might be, and be a man.

The damage is incalculable. Recalling our premise that the acts one does, the thoughts one thinks, register, one must fear this damage. Perhaps it is that the author cries out "I describe the dunghill because I hate it!" But continued and exclusive preoccupation with the dunghill does raise suspicions in the observer's mind. And the effect on our culture can be debasing and degrading. This vast dumping of refuse cannot fail to injure us. The apparently serious claim of some artists and critics that "the aim of modern art is to destroy art" raises two images in our minds; one, of the bird that fouls its own nest, and the other of the mentally ill patient who is treated (not cured!) by lobotomy. A part of the brain is destroyed, and the patient can return to useful life—but as less than a whole person. So this sick art, speaking to a sick clientele (one must suppose, although some of the sickness may be induced by the repetition of the formulas), proposes lobotomy. One sees, here, a madness of crowds induced by purveyors of a black mass.

The second aspect of the Humanists' responsibility, then, is to *be* Humanists; to be designers of progress rather than mere reporters, or passive consumers, or anchorites. They should be, and our culture needs them to be, where the action is: examining their society with the contact and objectivity of a judge; distinguishing symptoms of changes and weighing these with discrimination based on wide knowledge against lessons from the past and implications for the future, so that the ingredients of progress are clearly labeled and under constant quality control.

I see teachers in the Humanities as essential to the

governor function in the feedback loop of Figure 5.2. These teachers should inform their courses with an awareness of social and intellectual context; with a sense that what they teach does make a difference in the students' lives if it is relevant to their lives; with an embracing sense of learning. They should be sensitive to what is ignoble, and keep up the good fight for those basic virtues that have distinguished the best human beings—the great invariants of human life: honesty, integrity, sensitivity, imagination, just weight. They should be deeply aware that life requires directed effort; effort directed against the analogue of nature's entropy accumulation, that is against consistent, goal-centered degradation of behavior, and they should be alert critically to expose falsity, sham, ugliness, and sophistry in contemporary intellectual life; to restore the ancient criterion that a measure of the morality of an act is its disinterestedness, the extent to which it seeks its law outside of its objects, as Julien Benda puts it [6]: "that good is a decree of [man's] reason insofar as it is universal."

I would like to draw a few tentative analogies between some aspects of the Humanities and the Sciences. As I have said, man is a pattern-forming creature. He tends to classify experiences; to find relationships; and to generalize and abstract from these. This intellectual pathway is marked with monuments in the form of symbols. In the Humanities, some of these take the shape of unique utterances, fruit of the artist's intuition whether embodied in wood or stone, in sound or motion, in paint, in words, or whatever. These may, in analogy to Figure 3.9, be plotted close to a plane of experiences, *"E"* as in Figure 6.1. Others, such as concepts of beauty, truth, nobility, being invented, lie in a *"C"* field, and are connected to these by broken lines which symbolize ways of apprehending the concepts through experience with the unique exemplars and knowledge of how they came to be. I have not here utilized the operational rules, the double-line pathways of Figure 3.9, because it seems

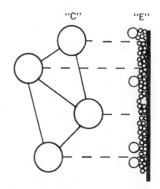

FIGURE 6.1 A field of knowledge and experience in the Humanitles. "E" Is the plane of experiences (see Figure 3.9) and "C" is the field of concepts.

to me that there is an essential difference between the Scientist's and the Humanist's approaches: there is a large cognitive component in the operational rules; and in these, a large component of the emotional and subjective. This is a significant difference, I believe: one that is to be valued and fostered. We must not insist that the same criteria of validation of theories and concepts be indiscriminately applicable in the Humanities and in the Sciences. There are differences between the two; differences of a very basic kind, as I have tried to show, which are to be valued for their contribution to the grand variety of life.

In both cases, Figures 3.9 and 6.1, the interconnections found among them, between the constructs and concepts, give them meaning. If the exemplars are unique, and all great art is unique, the rest being copied, they are nonetheless not isolated. I would think of the technologist of the Humanities as concerning himself chiefly with, or close to, the plane of experiences, and the critic and biographer as moving freely between the experiences and the concepts. The ultimate, the most subtle, the most intense, the universal, must be communicated in concrete terms. These communications will necessarily be unique utterances. But they are filled with meaning because they speak to the condition of so many of us, each within his living tomb. If we do not confuse uniqueness with isolation, and understand that it is isolation that evades meaning, then we can understand why it is that much alienated work seems to us so sterile: the cult of the absurd takes on a peculiar irony. And we are strengthened to understand the universality of the unique great work.

Certain highly speculative notions are suggested here. It seems to me that the extreme explicative critic, and the reductive biographer, are in the Humanities area the analogue of the logical positivist in the Scientific. They are *analytic* (elevated to a policy) and thus fragmenting and divisive. One almost hears the clank of mechanism—with one difference. There is the personal effect, in the exegesis practiced by such a critic on, say, a poem, which results in replacing the poet with the critic. The poem, perhaps even a single word in the poem, being the thing in isolation, becomes now the mirror from which is reflected the substituent critic. But as in Science, the old positivism has been discredited, and there is a slow swing in the direction of wholeness under the push of the concept of personal knowledge and the recognition of the decisive role of the Scientist himself, in scientific knowledge and experience; so there seems to be a movement, a mere suggestive note in the general shrillness, of a move away from this position in the Humanities.

What I would expect to find characterizing the well-tempered liberal Humanities is a sense of the connections between the imaginative and the functional aspects of their subjects. This depends in part on the recognition that the world is made up of, and the student's experience is of, things that may be ordered by reason as well as things that are necessary, and cannot be ordered, only persuaded, to use Jerome Bruner's figure [7]. The language of exposition and the language of insight are both needed; and both are respectable modes of communication.

Let me suggest some of the contributions that the well-tempered liberal Humanities might be expected to make to the student: To acquaint the student with the great values that have remained central issues for many people over long periods of time. To treat these with "high seriousness": values such as truth, beauty, goodness, nobility, power, love, duty, restraint. To expose the student to works (reminding him always, as an encouragement, that they are by *people*) wherein the best of form and content are embodied. To widen and sensitize the student's view of being within the wide range of experience that he is exposed to; the teacher, who went through this too, always lending a reassuring presence as needed. To help the student to understand that life is ambiguous and that the deliverances of the arts can be ambiguous without being confused; that it is possible to live with inconsistency at different levels or planes of abstraction without becoming fragmented. To show him that principles are important, and that adversity has its uses. To assist him to build all this into his own frame of reference; to make his own world. What we have in common in science and art, history and literature, says John Dillenberger [8], is the *making of worlds,* not the worlds.

One of the contributions to teachers of the Humanities that I would like to have made in this chapter is to offer encouragement—this on several counts. I have suggested elsewhere that there has been too much imitation of analytical aspects of science: as though all of science were data gathering and reporting. The fact seems to be that scientists generally choose problems that are soluble, and in public view at that. Everything else is left to the Humanist. He has all the hard, ambiguous, and essentially insoluble problems on his hands. Very well! This is to be accepted as a high compliment, and dealt with as adequately as possible.

Encouragement I would offer, too, to study science. Today science and technology are transforming our culture. The Humanist who has shut himself off, and who allows his students to shut themselves off, from the roots of this change has shut himself off from rich sources of inspiration. Think of the images with which he might speak to the minds and hearts of modern young persons if he knew enough science to give these images the ring of authenticity. Who knows what harmonies might be evoked at the impact of the new work in relativity theory, genetics, gravitation waves, or brain function upon the strings of the Humanist's sensitivity!

But the problem is also exigent. For as the competent Humanist withdraws from this duty to himself and his culture, as he abdicates this duty, a vacuum is created into which rush claimants of dubious repute. Degradation of the idea and practice of the Humanities may ensue. For modern students cannot be blamed for finding "modern" answers in the idiom more attractive than perhaps sounder ones couched in archaic language and arcane symbols. I urge the teacher in the Humanities to consider this matter most seriously, for present trends lead toward his destruction.

NOTES

1 I am indebted for the reflection of Goethe to Paul Horgan, Center for Advanced Studies, Wesleyan University. It comes from p. xvi of J. W. Goethe, *Italian Journey (1786–1788)*. Translated by W. H. Auden and Elizabeth Mayer (Pantheon Books, Inc., New York, 1962).

2 The Snow-Leavis affair is discussed by Martin Green, *Science and the Shabby Curate of Poetry: Essays about the two cultures* (W. W. Norton & Company, Inc., New York, 1965), pp. 12 ff. Further relevant material is, C. P. Snow, *The Two Cultures and The Scientific Revolution*. The Rede Lecture, 1959 (Cambridge University Press, London, 1959); F. R. Leavis, "The Significance of C. P. Snow" (the full text of the Richmond Lecture) in *The Spectator*, Number 6976, March 9, 1963, p. 297; and H. Margolis, "Intellectual Life in England: Leavis Views C. P. Snow; Boothby Views Leavis," in *Science, 135*:114 (1962).

3 Paul Horgan, "The Abdication of the Artist," in *Proceedings of the American Philosophical Society, 109*:267 (1965).

4 Katherine Anne Porter, "A Country and Some People I Love," in *Harper's Magazine, 231*, September 1963, p. 58.

5 Rebecca West, "A Grave and Reverend Book,"

in *Harper's Magazine,* February 1966, pp. 108 ff.;
see also p. 114.

6 The reference is to Julien Benda, *The Great
Betrayal.* Translated by Richard Aldington (Geo.
Routledge & Sons, Ltd., London, 1928), p. 99.

7 Jerome S. Bruner, *On Knowing: Essays for the
Left Hand* (Harvard University Press, Cambridge,
Mass., 1962).

8 John Dillenberger, *Seminar,* Danforth Foundation
Workshop in Liberal Arts Education, Colorado
Springs, Summer 1963.

7

A Scientific Theory of Value

In the experience of many people a cluster of related attitudes, false in origin and devastating in their consequences, lies at the basis of our major educational problems today. I have mentioned members of this cluster: fragmentation of the curriculum, alienation of students, disconnection between subjects which destroys meaning. I now treat this whole cluster on the basis of the scientific theory of value of Edward F. Haskell, with independent supporting work by Roger J. Williams [1] and others. The scientific approaches are new, yet their results validate and are validated by much that has been at the foundations of our great country: the teachings of our Founding Fathers; our Judaeo-Christian heritage; the works of truly great humanists who have given us insights to the natures of men. The advance is that these teachings may now be couched in operationally constant terms that enable us, as we shall see, to avoid if we wish the worst of our present semantical entanglements. But we must open our eyes and look clearly in order to see.

First, certain facts. A vast body of quantitative information exists about individual people: studies of size and other external properties, and studies of internal and external chemical and physiological properties. Some of this information has been gathered by Williams and skillfully put together. When he concludes that "You Are Extraordinary" he has an unexceptionable basis for this conclusion: the chance that any person is exactly like any other is infinitesimal and can be ignored; there is no likelihood that an average man exists, much less *the* average man.

For example, in a study made by the Mayo Clinic and reported by Williams, of some five thousand people with no known stomach disease, gastric juices varied at least one-thousandfold in pepsin content, and also in acid content. In other studies chemical factors—enzymes, hormones, blood sugar, and so on—have been found to vary widely, as also the sizes, shapes, positions of organs in the body. The blood vessels and nerve paths are tremendously dissimilar among people, as are shapes, sizes, markings of limbs, distribution of sensitive spots on the skin. People are unlike in their ability to sense and discriminate in taste, sight, hearing, smell. The number of different patterns that can be imagined in the connec-

KNOWLEDGE, EXPERIENCE, AND ACTION

tions between the more than a billion nerve cells in the brain—patterns that undoubtedly affect our behavior—is astronomical. Hundreds and hundreds of properties, when quantitatively studied, show a range of values. Sometimes the range is narrow: most people have five fingers per hand, but some have four and some six. Sometimes it is as wide as a thousandfold or more. When these scientifically validated findings are put together and examined statistically it is clear that even though there may be three-and-a-half billion people on the Earth the chances are vanishingly small that two of them are identical. The chances are negligible that there is a person with an average of every property—an average man. Every one of us is different. My uniqueness rests on data that certify also to the uniqueness of everyone else.

These findings give scientific support to what we all know: some people are better at some activities than others. A man with a very small stomach may have to eat much more often than another with a huge stomach—and he should not enter a pie-eating contest expecting to win. The sports pages of our newspaper confirm that people have different aptitudes, as do the psychological and other tests with which we bombard each other. Indeed, all this is so obvious that I have felt it necessary to emphasize it. For in spite of its obviousness we are bathed in a kind of egalitarian mush which falsifies values and may take from the individual his precious individuality, and with it that most intrinsic of his qualities, his existential responsibility.

Along with this wide variety in people's makeup—a variety based on hereditary, and physiological, and environmental factors—goes the fact that people are continually changing, and that not all are in the same state of development at any given time, nor do they develop at the same rates. It is perhaps no wonder that to grasp this fantastic variety desperate generalizations are made: "The average adult is . . . ." "The female teenager is . . . ." "All white men . . . ." "All black men . . . ." "All Protestants . . . ." "All Democrats . . . ."

To combat the evils, the class hatred, the race hatreds, the professional hatreds and jealousies that arise from idolization of these false generalizations we must teach the clear and present facts: all men are created unequal in the hereditary, physiological, and environmental factors that affect their lives. The variations are usually as great or greater within groups as between groups. Because of these differences each unique person may have something individual to offer. But how can such extraordinary variety be encompassed in a finite educational system? Only by discovering the invariants that allow us to translate between, and so live with, varieties of behavior, and by correlating educational processes to these. It is to the exposition of these invariants in a systematic manner that we turn next: to a brilliant formulation by the scientific generalist, Edward F. Haskell [2].

Consider interactions of all kinds between two persons; two groups of persons; one person and a group;

in short, two entities. We keep them distinct and in order by labeling one X and the other Y. We shall adopt the convention that X refers to the work factor and Y to the governor in a cybernetic analysis of the system. This usually means that Y is more controlling in some way than X, or is larger, or more powerful, and so forth. In any interaction where some particular process is being examined—as; for example, a learning process—Y affects

TABLE 7.1   The Table of Coactions between Two Entities, X and Y

		X		
	–	0	+	(x)
+	–, +	0, +	+, +	
Y 0	–, 0	0, 0	+, 0	
–	–, –	0, –	+, –	
(y)				

+ represents an acceleration or enhancement of the activity in question.
0 no effect.
– deceleration or diminution of the activity in question.
X the "weaker" entity. The effect on X is stated first in the coaction pair.
Y the "stronger" entity. The effect of Y is stated second in the coaction pair.

SOURCE: Edward F. Haskell, "Mathematical Systematization of 'Environment,' 'Organism,' and 'Habitat,' " in *Ecology, 21*:1 (1940).

TABLE 7.2 Decoding of Coaction Symbols

Symbol	Systematic Name	Translations, Common Names	Common Confusing Terms
+,+	Symbiosis	Cooperation, mutual aid	competition neutrality
0,+	Allotrophy*	Means "feeding the other"	neutrality
−,+	Predation	Exploitation of weak by strong	conflict parasitism competition neutrality
−,0	Amensalism*	Opposite of commensalism	neutrality
−,−	Synnecrosis	Mutual harm	conflict competition parasitism
0,−	Allolimy*	Means "starving the other"	neutrality
+,−	Parasitism	Exploitation of strong by weak	conflict commensalism neutrality
+,0	Commensal-ism	Feeding together	neutrality
0,0	Neutrality		

* New names. Where necessary to specify, Y is taken to be "stronger," or "more powerful," than X, as in assigning predation, parasitism, commensalism, and so forth.

X by increasing (+), not changing (0), or decreasing (−) the quality or quantity of what X is doing. Similarly, X affects Y as (+), (0), or (−). That is, suppose Y is a teacher. He might help the student to learn more or to learn better, or faster: the result for X is (+). At the same time, Y may be benefited by X, who may help him to become a better teacher; the effect for Y is (+). The possibilities that exist in any *coaction* between two entities are nine, found by cross-tabulation in Table 7.1. In Table 7.2 these are listed and the systematic names given them by biologists are attached. In three cases Haskell had to assign new names to the processes uncovered by this tabulation. Notice that in setting up Table 7.2 we have made the value-decision that constructive cooperation shall be called (+,+). From a purely logical point of view we could have defined (+,+) as an increase in conflict. The present decision is made to give the table its most useful empirical reference.

We know that there is infinite variability within types of coaction. To formulate this fact, Haskell maps the cross-table onto a coordinate system, as in Figure 7.1. Now, four of the types fall into the four quadrants: (+,+) in I; (−,+) in II; (−,−) in III; (+,−) in IV, and four others fall on the axes. Following convention, we write the values of the coactions with the X component, x, first (Figure 7.2). Now it is evident that any point in the coordinate system may be designated by giving its X and Y components (x,y). These may be stated only qualitatively, as, for example, in Figure 7.2 the point

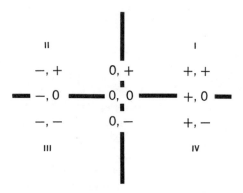

FIGURE 7.1 Coaction Compass. Mapping of the Coaction cross-table onto a coordinate system. From Haskell. See Chapter 7, Note 2.

(x,y) where x is clearly larger than y though both are (+). If, however, one can quantify the effects, then one can write in numerical values.

For example, letting Y represent the teacher and X the student, the symbiotic, cooperative coaction is (+,+). Suppose that the student is in class, unknown to the teacher, and he gains from the experience while having no influence on the teacher. This is (+,0). In a large class (X) containing one or two bright students (Y), the slow progress of the class may hold back the learning of the brighter ones, with resulting coaction (+,−). If the bright students are present but do not participate, and so have no effect on the class, the coaction may well be (0,−) in this respect. If a conflict situation develops between class and teacher so that learning time is

156   **KNOWLEDGE, EXPERIENCE, AND ACTION**

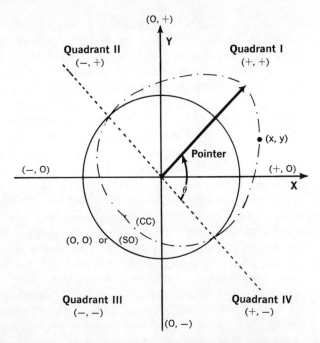

FIGURE 7.2 A Portion of the Periodic Coordinate System. The Co-actions of Tables 7.1 and 7.2 are interpreted geometrically, including the reference circle (0,0). The pointer indicates, in this Figure, the maximum $(+, +)$ coaction, where $|+x| = |+y|$. As the compass pointer swings through the angle θ, its tip traces out the cardioid-like figure (broken line). This line extends beyond the neutrality circle most markedly in Quadrant I, to indicate the cooperators' surplus; cuts the (0,0) circle at the midpoints of Quadrants II and IV; and falls inside the (0,0) circle to the left of the midpoint line (dotted line), showing the deficit produced by conflict. See Notes for references where the full significance of the diagram is presented and supported.

wasted and the teacher is frustrated, a (−,−) coaction is descriptive. Similarly for the rest of the coactions.

In the last column of Table 7.2 are listed some of the names given these coactions in common (and even scientific) usage. Both the presence of wide variations *within* a coaction *and the use of the same name for different coactions* lead to great confusion and semantical maladjustment in our lives. Consider the name "competition." There is the competition of a spelling-bee, for example. This is (+,+) competition, for both sides work hard to learn more words and surer spelling. A similar type of competition is found in most school athletic events. But there might be a competition between a bright (Y) and a dull (X) student for the teacher's time in class, and the bright one might well speed the lessons along so fast that he gains (+) at the expense (−) of the other. This would be a (−,+) coaction. Or, there is the case described above of (+,−). Both of these last could be moved, by small changes, toward (+,+) competition. Since all three are called competition, yet the results are clearly dissimilar, communication about these behaviors is difficult and confused. Add to this the deadly conflict wherein two entities (say labor and management) may in the name of free competition destroy each other (−,−) and the roster of confusion is complete.

This coordinate system, with refinements and additions that need not detain us, is named the Periodic Coordinate System by Haskell. Let a coaction be indicated by a pointer that extends from the origin to the applicable point, as illustrated in Figure 7.2. This pointer (a special kind of vector quantity) indicates the state of the coaction, and it will swing around as coaction changes, like a compass needle that points a state of affairs. Unlike a compass needle it may lengthen or shorten.

We are concerned in this chapter only with interactions between people and groups of people. For obvious reasons we do not discuss interactions between plants and animals, among themselves and with people, although the coaction compass is applicable to all interactions whatsoever, and in the education of a child or young adult the whole range would necessarily be studied. Here we raise two questions: a question of values, and a question about the application of these ideas to education.

To value something is to regard it highly, to look favorably upon it; to desire it if it is something one can have, or to emulate it if it is a way of behaving. Some things are valued as means, or instruments, toward an end (for example, money, or power, or knowledge); others for themselves, for their intrinsic worth (for example, truth, beauty, goodness). Yet even here there is an end in view: a sense of fitness, of satisfaction with true or good or beautiful things. With respect to coaction, we regard $(+,+)$ as more valuable both instrumentally and intrinsically than $(-,-)$ and, indeed, the degree of positive is correlated with positive value, and actions which are classified as $(+,+)$ are better, more moral, more ethically justified than those negative in nature. We must ask, however, on what are such judgments based? How are they justified? and Why do people behave in so many degrees of less good and of evil ways?

Basically, I suppose, survival and betterment of the species in the sense of its fitness to the environment is an ultimate good, at the physical level; reverence for life at the ethical (Schweitzer). In the earliest days of mankind people hunted, and scraped the Earth with digging sticks. They led a precarious existence. Survival depended on $(+,+)$ cooperation within the group. There was always some kind of social structure, with children doing certain things, young adults doing others, and so on, and a leader who might be male or female, and usually older and wiser than the others. Individual differences probably could not be catered to unless they had special value to the group, as superior hunting ability or inventiveness in emergencies might have. As people learned to live together in larger groups, this required subordination of deadly conflict $(-,-)$ and the more destructive forms of parasitism and predation within the society. It required, too, $(+,+)$ cooperation with the environment: learning to fertilize fields and rotate crops; to breed cattle and other useful animals; to control the ecology of the land. Broadly speaking—and it is clearly evident that mankind did progress toward our present state where in the great industrial societies nearly everyone eats regularly and has a chance for a share of the World's energy—cooperative interactions, $(+,+)$, and those parts of quadrants

160

II and IV wherein (+) outweighs (−) in magnitude, have *far* outweighed the negative ones. This analysis of inter-actions, which removes the confusions about terms like competition and conflict (there are whole ranges of coac-tions to which these names have been applied) points the basic error in the assertion, apparently believed by large numbers of people, that "all history is the history of class conflict." This cannot have been so. For conflict (−,−) destroys, and so do the coactions (−,+) and (+,−) where (−) outweighs (+). And we can see the fruits of cooperation evident all about us.

The matter deserves a further word, since it is one of the problems in the cluster mentioned above. As a society becomes more complex, evolves from primitive to civilized, it inevitably develops a class structure. This is neither inherently bad nor good: it is a consequence of increased complexity. For people are different, and some can do things needed by the society better than others, and so are likely to be valued more for, and obtain more satisfaction in, doing these things. Others do other things. Of course there are inequities, and advantages taken, and privilege, and so forth. But the fact remains that there are classes. Moreover, in our society sociologists have found and clearly identified them. Lloyd Warner and his associates [3] found six classes in Yankee City: they were even biologically marked off by the fact that members of the class by far most frequently married within the class, although there was some mobility between classes.

The fact is, as Haskell points out, that we are quite

aware of classes, and that the existence of class can be quite noticeable in cooperation: the leader and members of a hunting band; the managers and workers in a profit-sharing company. A choleric, or melancholic follower may not notice it. He will screen out such recognition for it contradicts his value-premise "I am never a follower." But we must be very careful to reject the Marxist premise that the only relation between the classes is that of conflict. This makes it impossible to become aware of, and to increase, class cooperation. We must strengthen our self-confidence in our Country and our heritage. Our citizens are by and large the best-off in the World because of the dominantly class-cooperative $(+, +)$ value premises in our cultural (religious, humanistic, and scientific) heritage. Other new countries have as many resources; but where their ideologies are conflict-oriented $(-, -)$ the whole culture is sick and unproductive of the goods of life. Where some of these countries have begun to turn toward the $(+, +)$ value premise, they have simultaneously and indeed inevitably begun to prosper. This requires intelligent class consciousness, recognition of class cooperation, and the fostering of cooperation.

Anthropologists have pointed out that the kinds of people chosen as leaders in a society correspond in their temperaments to the society's dominant and deviant value premises at any given time. This is documented by Ruth Benedict [4] and confirmed by Clyde Kluckhohn. Our cybernetic analysis in Chapter 5 shows the inner

162

mechanism of this: the goals of the system, as we saw (its dominant and deviant value premises), are the consequence of the (ethical) stance of its governor. They, however, affect the output as well as the habitat of the system which by retroaction affects the governor; the system itself may change its governor. We turn, then, to the behaviors of people. Again, I present Haskell's analysis but only in abbreviated, categorical, and largely undocumented form, and sufficient only to carry us forward to the next step: application to education.

With respect to their typical behavior patterns (their temperaments) people fall into four broad classes. We do not, of course, accept Hippocrates' theory of temperaments, but he was a good observer, and his classification is valid. It is interesting and objectively validating that Ivan Pavlov [5] could not find a better set of terms under which to classify the behaviors of the hundreds of dogs he studied in the laboratory than the terms given by Hippocrates to the corresponding human temperaments. The four classes fall naturally into the four quadrants of the Coaction Compass.

Psychologists have coded behaviors in ways that imply the interaction in personality of two traits. The resulting coactions are given different names depending on the intensity of their manifestations. They are mapped onto the coaction coordinate system by Haskell as follows. The *phlegmatic* is $(+, +)$. The phlegmatic temperament is such that the person accepts the role of leader or of follower, as the occasion demands, with equanimity: he is strong in the traits of submission (X) and domination (Y); he is not upset by being made chairman of a committee, or a department, nor is he disturbed by giving someone else the chance to run things. This may lead to the misconception that the phlegmatic temperament is lacking in feeling. The *choleric* temperament is weak in submission and strong in domination; that is, $(-, +)$. Such people are aggressive; they want to run things. If they don't get to be captain they may sulk. The *melancholic* is weak in both traits $(-, -)$. The *sanguine* is strong in submission and weak in domination $(+, -)$.

When these traits are balanced in each temperament to a certain intensity the result is normal behavior. Increase the intensity and the behavior moves into the classification "neurotic." When Karen Horney's [6] classification of human neuroses is recoded by Haskell in coaction terms the four classes fall into the quadrants: the *choleric* responds to situations by "moving against others" in Horney's terms; the *melancholic,* by moving away from people; the *sanguine,* by moving toward others; and the *phlegmatic* is classified as "well." (Being a psychopathologist her official classification of neuroses extended only to the three deviant or sick [in her culture] types of behavior.) Phlegmatic persons $(+, +)$ are capable of moving either against or toward others without being upset by either necessity.

When the intensity is further increased, the behavior enters the realm of the psychotic. Here it is clear that paranoia is the expression of $(-, +)$; schizophrenia, of

TABLE 7.3   Personality States

Coaction	Normal Temperament	Neurotic State	Psychotic State
(+,+)	Phlegmatic	Well	Genius
(−,+)	Choleric	Moving against	Paranoia
(−,−)	Melancholic	Moving away from	Schizophrenia
(+,−)	Sanguine	Moving toward	

SOURCE: Edward F. Haskell, *Assembly of the Sciences,* Vol. 2.

(−,−). In this intensity (+,+) is not only well, but outstandingly strong. Haskell names it genius, since George T. Lodge [7] found this combination of traits outstanding in Nobel Prize winners. These relationships are gathered in Table 7.3.

We remarked, earlier, that people vary in hereditary, physiological, and environmental factors that affect their lives. That these ways of behaving (and within each temperament-quadrant there is room for infinite variation) are in part hereditary is within the knowledge of all of us who discuss the traits of our ancestors, and friends and their ancestors. It is clearly demonstrated in animals. Sheepdogs are bred for (+,+); they obey their master, and they herd their sheep. They are strong in submission and domination. Watchdogs (−,+) take orders from none but a master—sometimes even growling at him —and defend their territory aggressively. A melancholic dog (−,−) withdraws: it slinks around, tail between legs, and cringes at any friendly overture. The sanguine dog is bred as a pet (+,−). It makes friends with everyone. The hereditary pattern is not as clear with people, perhaps, but it is well recognized by psychologists.

The environmental factor plays a role also; to revert to the simpler cases: a choleric dog that bites other dogs and growls at people tends to be bitten and ill-treated in return. By positive feedback it may become more choleric. The slinking and withdrawn dog is no pleasure to anyone, and people withdraw from it, or abuse it, causing it to withdraw further. The pet loves everyone and is loved in return: it becomes confirmed in its pleasing ways.

Applied to persons, we see the same feedback operating. One of our grand traits, which we share with the British and some other nations, is our development of team play and work. This begins at an early age and accentuates (+,+) interactions of all kinds. Behavior of the (−,+) type tends to drive people away, and the aggressive person of this kind must either change or become disliked. His natural prey are the (+,−) people. These people, when their behavior is somewhat intense, have an appealing humility and defenselessness, attributing to others their feelings of friendliness. When people are hostile and brutal toward them they feel that the fault must lie in them, and by positive feedback they may become more helpless, more self-abusing. They tend to be oversolicitous and continually more vulnerable to exploitation by choleric or paranoid persons who in turn become intensified in their behavior.

This presentation has been much too categorical and oversimplified. It should be qualified in many ways. For example, it is not easy to distinguish the paranoid of quadrant II, when his traits fall close to the $(-)X$ axis from the paranoid schizophrenic just across the line. However, enough has been described to suggest that Haskell's work supports a theory of value of the greatest importance to education.

Let us first accept as deeply true that not all people are equal; part of this unequalness was conferred upon them in the encounter of a sperm and an egg in their mother's womb: this sperm, not that one; this egg, not one from an earlier or later ovulation. Nor was this entirely under the control of their parents, for while it is possible to prevent fertilization; while good health of parents can be maximized; while it is possible to damage sperm or egg by drugs and disease, there are also changes that are fortuitous: favorable or unfavorable mutations outside the will or negligence of any parent. But there is also a part of their unequalness that they and we can do something about: the environmental part. Here coaction theory also has something to say. Some people are geniuses in science, in the arts, in sport, in interpersonal relations, and so on. Most of us are not. Some of us—even geniuses—are extremely poor at some things. But the qualities of whatever type that are useful to mankind are best fostered in an environment dominated by positive values. Here a man who finds his métier as street cleaner would be encouraged to be the best person he can be. Work would be found for him, and he would be valued as a member of his community. In early days in the best circumstances each person in a village was known and able to be an individual, valued for what he could do as well as how he did it. One spoke in that idiom of "a calling."

In Figure 7.2 there is plotted a dotted line that bisects quadrants II and IV. Along this line the magnitudes of $(+)$ and $(-)$ in a quadrant are equal, and cancel. A circle, representing the reference axis from which coactions are plotted, cuts this line at points where $|+|=|-|$. The vertical lines, here, are conventional, and mean "the magnitude of". The circle, being a reference, is neutral with respect to the quadrants: it is what would be observed if X and Y did not affect each other. This is a base line. Then, to discover that a teacher and a student (for example) have improved in their interaction $(+,+)$ one must find that the result, however measured or estimated, falls in quadrant I, that is, outside of this reference circle; that is, at larger values of x and y than would be the case (x_0, y_0) without the coaction. Similarly, when two coacting entities have injured each other $(-,-)$ the result of the process must fall within the circle, in quadrant III. The dashed cardiod-like figure shows the kind of plot that would be expected if the units along the X and Y axes were the same. If the units are not the same (the teacher, Y, may value proficiency in his subject in a way different from his student, X) then the curve may be skewed, if it can be made at all precise. In any event, coactions can be evaluated in quality and estimated in quantity, and by the nature of the case, positive, net constructive coactions fall on the quadrant I side of the line bisecting quadrants II and IV, outside of the (0,0) reference axis, and destructive, conflictive coactions fall on the quadrant III side, inside of the (0,0) reference axis. The former clearly maps what the moral philosopher, Braithwaite [8], has called a cooperator's surplus; the latter we would call a conflictor's deficit. Evidence in support of this theory of coaction is found throughout nature, from the controlled experiments of Gause [9] and Witt with paramecia, through ecological studies of all kinds, to political behavior.

The clear facts are that cooperation builds and conflict destroys. Inevitably. And the effects last even unto the third and fourth generations. When people behave in a choleric, or any other way, it is almost always because they believe that it pays off for them. Eric Hoffer has documented the variety of such behavior in his *True Believer* [10], and Chad Walsh in *From Utopia to Nightmare* [11]. The choleric who gets his own way is confirmed in his aggression. He may manage bread and circuses for his dupes, or visions of a better world; but by the nature of the way things are, by the nature of the actual, ineluctable substrate of existence, he will fail. For conflict does not build good. (There may be local appearances that it does, or propaganda to generate appearances, but Nature just does not behave that way, and we had better take a leaf out of the scientist's notebook and ask her, and pay attention to what she says.)

The Coaction Compass is a kind of animated map of the way things are: it distinguishes not only the broad categories of value, the $(+)$ from the $(-)$ coactions, but provides in its spatial extent for an infinity of variations. There can be in principle a coaction pointer for every kind of process, and the sum of these (treated perhaps as vector arrows) might then define the state of the system in question. People with $(+,+)$ temperaments, parents, community leaders, church and national leaders, seeing fluctuations from a generally $(+,+)$ value-goal, will realize, when they study in these terms, that words like "conflict" and "cooperation" are multiordinal. Thus, as Haskell points out, conflict among predators or parasites decreases destruction; cooperation between them destroys. As he says, the algebra of the web-of-life is immensely complex and sophisticated. Far more so, indeed, than this chapter can show. But our ability to discriminate has been eroded by false doctrines. The cultural relativist teaches that since different cultures have been found, with widely different value-premises, the "patterns of life which mankind has created for itself from the raw materials of existence" are all equally valid. This equates the ferociously negative Dobu and Kwakiutl cultures with the dominantly positive Hopi and Zuñi as equally valid. Yet the former are dying out, while the latter are making their way even under most difficult circumstances. This type of presumed "objectivity" has led to value-relativism, or as Haskell terms it, value-promiscuity. (The term is meant to recall Toynbee's findings that this type of valueless system has correlated with the decline and fall of civilizations. It is particularly noticeable when leaders withdraw from their communities.)

In today's world we see massive demonstrations of this truth. A country, in so far as it bases its value-premises and its dominant behavior on doctrines that would be indicated negative by the Coaction Compass *cannot* realize for its citizens its potential. For example, those countries that profess and practice Marxist, Leninist, Stalinist, and Maoist doctrines repeatedly have set up great plans that have failed to meet their professed objectives (*true* pie-in-the-sky). Yet they are far from lacking in natural resources. This is documented for the Soviet states by such studies as Leites' *The Operational Code of the Politburo* [12], and Paloczi-Horvath's *The Facts Rebel* [13]. One need only encode the doctrines of Marx and Stalin, for example, to see the dominant conflict-orientation. One must observe that much of this conflict-oriented doctrine is now specifically for export, while internally there is increasing recognition of the values of individual contributions (enterprise) and the uses of many-faceted cooperation. The communist line exports value-promiscuity and cultural-relativism for their confusion-producing and destructive effects, but *within* the Soviet Union neither is tolerated.

One tremendous virtue of the Coaction Compass

formulation of value-theory is that it becomes possible through it to lift the discussion of values from the emotional quagmires and semantical jungles which entrap such discussion: one speaks in clear terms of (+), (0), and (−), and has available degrees of qualities and quantities of coactions. Then it becomes possible to talk with scientists and others in other cultures in terms that evade the emotional, the propagandistic web of connotations festooning our common terms. Then perhaps it can become evident to enough of us on this Space-Ship Earth in enough countries that we must either *truly* live together (+,+) or we shall surely die together (−,−). The theory further shows how negative may be changed toward positive coaction, and the process recognized as it occurs; cybernetics shows how to arrange it. But above all we must not expect instantaneous results. The sins that have been committed can be expiated. The powerful virtue that may achieve this is inherent in well-planned, scientifically organized "expiation" that tangibly brings "forgiveness". Therefore, we must be tenacious, wise, and strong in our belief in these positive grand doctrines of our heritage. And we must teach them.

In summary, and application to education, then, people are all different from each other in some ways. Nevertheless, they may be classed broadly under temperaments which code their dominant behavior pattern as phlegmatic (+,+), choleric (−,+), melancholic (−,−), and sanguine (+,−), while leaving room for wide variation in each. When these behaviors are of normal intensity they provide the rich and useful variety that we all experience. But when the negatively biased ones are at neurotic or psychotic levels they become dangerous and potentially destructive. Moreover, any temperament, if successful, can by positive feedback be reinforced until it becomes of abnormal intensity. This is one statement of the old truth that power corrupts, and it provides cybernetic insight to the wisdom of checks and balances: but naïvely organized checks can stultify.

All the properties of a culture are linked, and the state of the culture is a property of its dominant value-premises, that is, of its dominant coaction. It is therefore essential to maintain the highest values in all aspects of a culture; not to think that it doesn't matter if only a small percentage of the populace use drugs, or distribute pornographic literature, or indulge in criminal acts. It is of the highest importance for the society, since by the retroaction of example, and teaching, these destructive and evil behaviors can escalate. Moreover, the society selects its leaders according to its own value-premises, and thus by retroaction can foster negative coaction or positive. We must therefore educate ourselves to be able to discriminate between good and evil. If evil is regarded as sickness, then strong prompt sanctions must be viewed as therapy, and not omitted. We should with equal tenacity recognize good, and reinforce it with just rewards. The victims of evil acts should have at least equal chance at cure as the criminal.

Those cultures, or societies, thrive that live through

positive dominant value-premises based on cooperation, brotherly love (brothers may freely disagree and still love each other), earned mutual trust, ability to be disinterested (it is false doctrine to preach that "if you're not with me you're against me" for this ignores the umpire function and the function of judge, and leaves *no* alternative to conflict), ability to discriminate good from evil on the basis of fact coupled with intolerance of evil, and on concern for the individual as a unique and intrinsically valuable person. One has only to look at the World clearly to confirm this; to part the curtain of sophistries, semantic juggling with words, and general communications-noise that hide the truth. Those cultures with dominant negative value-premises, in so far as they practice them, are doomed by their own doctrines. When they make a great leap forward, as Haskell puts it, it is over the cliff.

Thus we must teach values from kindergarten on. Children should learn to discriminate between all nine coactions, and to code utterances as well as acts in these operationally constant terms. They should learn how people can be unequal and yet free; unequal in abilities yet equal in opportunities. The seeds of value-promiscuity must find no ground on which to grow.

It becomes evident, then, how an education can be made relevant to the student's life: values must be returned to a central position. A course taught in the presence of the Coaction Compass and Periodic Coordinate System immediately gains a new dimension. For the Periodic Coordinate System is the *invariant-relation* which makes it possible to recognize and evaluate the most diverse behaviors; and to translate from person to person, from culture to culture, what without it is obscure, confused, and a source of misunderstanding.

NOTES

1 The work of Roger J. Williams to which I refer is *Free and Unequal: The Biological Basis of Individual Liberty* (University of Texas Press, Austin, Texas, 1953); *Biochemical Individuality: The Basis for the Genetotrophic Concept* (John Wiley & Sons, Inc., New York, 1956); *You Are Extraordinary* (Random House, Inc., New York, 1966).

2 The work of Edward F. Haskell to which I refer is "Mathematical Systematization of 'Environment,' 'Organism,' and 'Habitat,'" in *Ecology*, 21:1 (1940); "A Clarification of Social Science," in *Main Currents in Modern Thought*, 7:45 (1949); *Assembly of the Sciences*, I: *Scientia Generalis*; II, *Res Cogitans*; III, *Calculemus!* (Unpublished.)

In Figure 7.2 a portion of Haskell's comprehensive Periodic Coordinate System is presented. I have simplified it because to do it full justice would require three volumes. The essential points are that interactions above and to the right of the diagonal axis that bisects Quadrants II and IV are net positive, and those below and to the left are net negative. The "scalar zero" circle (S0) is the reference, or base line, from which co-actions are plotted. It represents neutrality (0,0), and has the same value everywhere. The heavy pointer, by its length relative to the radius of the

176

S0 circle, indicates the magnitude of a coaction. By the nature of the way things are, the length of this pointer changes with its direction relative to the dotted line bisecting quadrants II and IV. Measuring from this dotted line, the angle of the pointer in Figure 7.2 is $\theta = 90°$. Here the values of $+x$ and $+y$ are maximal. Where the cardioid-like figure (CC) traced by the pointer cuts the S0 circle, namely at $\theta = 0$ and $\theta = 180°$, the magnitudes of x and y are equal, but the signs are opposite, so the net coaction is zero.

It is found by applying this conceptual scheme to experimental data that there is a bias in nature: coactions of the net positive kind are correlated to evolutionary improvement. Complexity of organism-habitat interactions increase, with concomitant increased organization. Coactions of the net negative kind are correlated to retrogressions and disintegrations. Experiment and coaction theory tell us that nature is biased toward the $(+, +)$ coaction. This offers a scientific basis for valuation.

3 W. Lloyd Warner, J. O. Low, Paul S. Lunt, and Leo Srole, *Yankee City* (Yale University Press, New Haven, Conn., 1963), a one-volume abridgement of the five-volume Yankee City Series.
4 Ruth Benedict, *Patterns of Culture*. A Mentor Book (The New American Library, Inc., New York, 1948 [Houghton Mifflin Company, Boston, Mass., 1934]).

5 Ivan Pavlov, *Conditioned Reflexes* (Oxford University Press, London, 1928), Chap. 17.

6 Karen Horney, *Our Inner Conflicts: A Constructive Theory of Neurosis* (W. W. Norton & Company, Inc., New York, 1945).

7 George T. Lodge, in Haskell's *Assembly of the Sciences,* Vol. III.

8 R. B. Braithwaite, *Theory of Games as a Tool for the Moral Philosopher* (Cambridge University Press, London, 1955), p. 20.

9 G. F. Gause, *The Struggle for Existence* (Williams & Wilkins Co., Baltimore, Md., 1934); *Vérifications expérimentales de la théorie mathématique de la lutte pour la vie.* No. 277 in Actualités Scientifiques et Industrielles (Hermann & Cie., Paris, 1935).

10 Eric Hoffer, *The True Believer: Thoughts on the Nature of Mass Movements* (Harper & Row, Publishers, New York, 1951).

11 Chad Walsh, *From Utopia to Nightmare* (Harper & Row, Publishers, New York, 1962).

12 Nathan Leites, *The Operational Code of the Politburo.* A publication of research by The Rand Corporation (McGraw-Hill Book Company, New York, 1951).

13 George Paloczi-Horvath, *The Facts Rebel: The Future of Russia and the West* (Secker & Warburg, London, 1964).

8

One Culture, Indivisible (with Variety Enough for All)

The Sphere of Knowledge and Experience, Figure 4.3, has room for every intellectual discipline that is taught in college. It implies that all knowledge and experience are connected at some level. Moreover, since knowledge is for use, as a guide to action, and since it is in the realm of action that moral problems arise, problems whose rationale is ethics, we see that by implication knowledge, experience, action, moral problems, and ethics are all interwoven in the vast nexus of relationships embodied in the metaphor of Figure 4.3. It is the case, also, that each discipline, each item in each discipline, takes on added meaning for us as we increasingly recognize and understand its connections within the whole. Thus meaning emerges from the knowledge and experience comprised by all the deliverances of our senses, the operations of our mind, the intimations of our soul. Lambent or dark intimations of prophesy and revelation; clear or murky perceptions in science, art, and technology; gamuts wherein a range of juxtaposed opposites are bracketed by unattainable absolutes, where there is no truth without a taint of falsity, no good without attendant evil, no beauty without some ugliness, yet ordered by the beckoning, jussive, perfection of ideals; in short, ambiguities, paradoxes, and complementarities of life—all find a place in this metaphor.

It is this great nexus of meanings, this web of connectedness, that is the frame of reference, and context, of education. We can grasp it only in imagination. We can each be technically competent in only a small part. Yet each of us can be a part of others in his conceptual grasp of his segment of the whole, so that we can be one in the body of this Alma Mater—each a bearer of meaning. This, in epitome, has been the theme of these chapters, and the vision of one culture indivisible, with variety enough for all.

Once more we turn to thoughts about the roles of students, teachers, and their subjects in the educational process. We again speak discursively of what should be handled as a whole. Achievements at the conceptual level, changing the ways of thinking, are far more difficult and much slower to bring about than those at the institutional level. The latter require only money. What is needed is to alter many of our ways of thinking and to encourage explicit application of these ideas so as to alter ways of behaving. For the basic principles stated in Chapter 2 are, I think, widely accepted. That there is wide consensus in these principles implies that encouragement by example is what is chiefly needed, so that in consideration of the acts and gifts of others we, too, are encouraged to act and give.

Mr. Christopher Givan, a student formerly in my course in physical science at Yale, wrote me as follows, after listening to a talk on curricular problems:

> A course should say: "Your prime duty as a student in this college is to fulfill yourself by being most yourself. I am a course in Oriental Art. I can tell you this and this about Chinese paintings. Does it help you? Are you feeling better about yourself as a person? Are your day-to-day experiences and concerns for things you see, ideas you hear, situations you notice in Civil Rights bills or an unhappy roommate, becoming clearer to you? I hope in listening to me as a course, and memorizing Chinese art you will feel fuller as a person and be more aware of yourself than when you first entered this course." Or, an Instructor in the course should say: "This is a course in physics. I represent the University's goals. I must impose certain demands on you. The Administration and I are most concerned that you develop as a person. We do not want blue-books or grades to be your goals. What we want is proof that by taking physics you have become less timid in the face of life's possibilities. We want proof that you are assimilating the facts as taught in this physics

course with your own ideas. Write me a paper [to show in what ways] this course is contributing something permanent to your entire spectrum of experience."

Here we have the statement of a sensitive and intelligent man saying what his education should do for him. His courses should help him to fulfill himself by being most himself in the important sense of changing himself by actualizing his potential; to be fuller and more aware of himself; to be less timid in the face of life's possibilities; to have his spectrum of experience enlarged; in Biblical terms, to be reborn: not "Be yourself" but "To thine own self be true," which is to change yourself so as to be better. These are not goals to be achieved in any absolute sense. But the student asks that the college enhance what may already have been begun; prepare his further maturation; keep open and enrich the avenues of personal development.

How can courses do this? Certainly not by themselves, but in the interplay of student and subject mediated by the teacher, in large lecture courses, or of student and teacher mediated by the subject, in small courses. No teaching can be legislated by listing courses. The process is clearly technological in nature. It is the application to practice, in the case of *this* student, of the subject; of the teacher's wide knowledge and skills; and of all the other habitat factors that are germane. It needs re-emphasis, I believe, that there are teachers who *really* know more than their students. There *really* exist older and more sophisticated people whose equals students are *not,* and from whom they can learn. Along with an accumulation of substantive knowledge—an equity which most students cannot have since it takes years of time to accumulate and develop it—these people have something else: judgment, and some sense of history.

Let me sketch a few ways that courses and teachers may help to these ends. Where does the student find examples that help him to fuller awareness and to fulfillment of himself and of others? Primarily, I would say, in great literature—poetry, novels, plays, biographies of scientists and humanists, and sacred writings. Psychologists are beginning to be of some help, here, and will assume more effective roles, I am sure, but by the nature of psychology as a science, it is difficult for it to deal with the ineffable, with the resolution of ambiguities and the reconciliation of opposites that we turn to great literature for. The student needs to be put on the track, here, at the very least. He needs to be turned toward the view, and even told what to see, at first; what to listen for and what to hear.

The teacher must exercise discretion here. The literature and sacred writings he chooses should, it seems to me, foster the habits of holistic thinking; of process-thinking; of thinking of consequences; or it should serve to show the effects of failure of such teaching. What freshness this could introduce; what relevance to the student's life. Along with such interpretive guidance by the teacher must go some encouragement of the student to work with the medium, so that he can have first-hand experience of the intransigence of matter and word; and he should be encouraged to do his own interpretation, so that he can experience the elusiveness of ideas and the duplicity of words and other media. This is, indeed, the fundamental purpose of laboratory work and term papers.

I have said a number of times that the liberal arts college needs to oppose some present graduate school trends. The reason for this should now be clearer. The student needs several years in which to find himself. He needs to relate himself to his heritage as well as to his times. He needs to sort and firm up his beliefs; to strengthen his moral and intellectual framework. This must all be well begun before he starts to specialize. Specialization, as I have said, is utterly essential today. It is a source of power. But the student must be *prepared* to receive this power, so that cognition *and* emotion together may guide action. Then power may become united with virtue.

When I say that the liberal arts college must oppose some graduate school trends, I mean *oppose*—not merely *resist*. I do not, however, mean that some even-handed administrator must preside over the just distribution of rewards and punishments, to keep those "bad" graduate school people in line. The only fruitful opposition that I see possible must come from the undergraduate teachers and students themselves. They must meet the challenge of the graduate school program by doing the right things with their own curriculum. Then both will be gainers.

KNOWLEDGE, EXPERIENCE, AND ACTION

In talking with students and teachers, the impression comes through strongly that it is only when he has started his major that the student emerges from the "sophomore slump" and becomes goal-directed, hard-working, and relatively happy with his lot. Some teachers and administrators have read into this a license to begin the major in earlier years—to the extreme, indeed, that in some colleges the major (for example, in chemistry, or mathematics) is considered to begin in secondary school, so that the student begins to take "graduate courses" by his junior year.

As I evaluate the results of such thinking, I find that many students are injured in this process: I have seen them emerge maimed in intellect, personality, and spirit. I have seen them emerge with a fostered arrogance too ignorant to recognize its own stupidity. This is a real danger, that there is bred a kind of narrow intellectual arrogance that is destructive: the ultimate academic sin, ignorance of ignorance.

What then of the clear evidence that beginning the major often brings the student to life? I think that our findings can yield at least a tentative answer: it is only in the major that the student begins consciously to find meaning to his college work. Here he sees the relations between parts of the subject; he finds himself related to the subject as a participator and contributor to it; he is told, perhaps for the first time, why he is asked to take certain courses and not others. There is released in him what was always there—the willingness to put forth the greatest effort. Both he and the work have meaning: they are worthy of being believed in. But alas, if he has been brought up in the typical preprofessional mold, other problems become exacerbated. For as he begins to specialize, so may be "filtered out" or "tuned out" knowledge of the rest of the world. Those facts and theories which do not fit the paradigm of his narrow specialty are first ignored, then not seen. He becomes ever more crippled and ever more sure in his self-fulfilling way that he has some license to divine standing in his field (and not always with a small "d").

If this analysis is substantially correct, as I believe it to be, then it implies that the earlier years are not performing as they should. The sophomore slump is a sign. It is diagnostic of the disease of the college: fragmentation of knowledge and experience; separation and opposition of the cognitive and emotional parts of life, and their divorce from action. Effectively to oppose the further penetration of the specialist attitude into the undergraduate curricula, the teachers and students must heal the intellectual schism that there exists. It will be widened and deepened and exacerbated by the further penetration of the specialist attitude.

I believe that the use of concepts of the breadth and integrity embodied in Figures 3.9, 4.3, and 7.2 in planning courses and curricula *and in teaching them* can go far toward correcting this state of affairs. We need to show connections while preserving variety, and we need to help the student to relate himself, as I said, to his heritage and his contemporary world. The solution for

KNOWLEDGE, EXPERIENCE, AND ACTION

his students lies in the hands of each teacher: he should teach his course in the light of all courses; as a paradigm of knowledge and experience; of the union of thought, feeling, and behavior.

This brings me to the matter of timidity in the face of life's possibilities. Let me relate a small example of dealing with this. I like to urge Humanities majors who take my course to buy a slide rule (they are now quite inexpensive), and I teach those who so wish to use it for the few types of calculations we make. The results have been striking in some cases. The man with an engineering roommate, who whips out his slide rule coolly to calculate, has surely gained the upper hand over one of life's possibilities, and his timidity is further decreased if, through rather deep knowledge of some limited scientific subject coupled with seeing relationships to many fields, he can hold his own with his roommates in midnight discussions. Objective evidence: one sees this man strolling between classes with the slide rule showing casually out of his inside jacket pocket.

To become less timid: I would like to discuss this under three related headings: doubt, belief, and ambiguity.

Judge Learned Hand is said to have remarked "when the ignorant are taught to doubt, they know not what to believe." This is the theme of many a freshman year.

The emotionally and especially intellectually immature student comes to college. He is ignorant; he knows he is ignorant, and he is told so on many occasions. Often he wears a badge of office. (Please don't accuse me of urging that we do away with "freshman beanies." These are usually harmless and perhaps even are important in lending a touch of humor to, or in giving a sense of a cadre to, the harassed student.) He is fair game for the one-upmanship of the upperclassman. A great deal of this has educational value, firming up his recognition that words are pliant tools.

But he enters the classroom and draws a teacher whose main objective seems to be, whatever the subject, from English or history to biology or physics, to break down any fixed beliefs, intellectual, moral, religious, with which the student has come. Now it is important that the student be taught to doubt. A degree of skepticism based on logic and a clear eye is healthful in the extreme. But only is this admissible in teaching if at the same time the ignorance of the student is corrected by teaching meaningful courses: courses connected to a sound intellectual, moral, and sacred framework, and only if the student is led, and explicitly encouraged, to reconstruct a sounder belief: a framework which is the stronger because he has gone through the discipline and turmoil of building it himself.

Those who have gained the confidence of freshmen, and have talked with them, will confirm, I am sure, what I have repeatedly observed, that the more intelligent and sensitive ones can be shattered by this experience; they can lose interest in college work which seems shallow, disconnected, and meaningless, and they can drop out, wandering into military service, jobs of

188

one kind or another, or pure vagrancy. It is easy to destroy—*always*; it is difficult to construct. No teacher should take away more than he gives in return, and his gift should be of the highest quality that he can command, and flowing over.

Some of the teachers to whom I refer are quite honest, if ignorant and imperceptive. They even believe in being "objective" with a result, as Robert Rankin once remarked [1], that an objective professor may leave his student shivering in the breeze of his open mind. My experience in teaching physical science is that the single topic of most concern to students is the impact of their courses (all their courses, not just physical science) upon their beliefs. They respond in wonderful and often quite surprising ways to a sympathetic ear, a judicious question, a word of encouragement, and an example.

My second point has to do broadly with beliefs, and bears upon the duty of the college to relate the student, intellectually, morally, emotionally, to his heritage *and* to the contemporary scene. It is, of course, intimately related to the previous point. Put baldly, a central problem of our time is that we preach one behavior, and practice another in many areas of our culture. For example, in college, we preach the primary importance of good teaching, knowing that without it the interpretation of knowledge and experience to the young would fail, and the springs of our culture dry up, yet we give greatest rewards to research, particularly in the science areas, and thus to acquiring new knowledge—assimilated or merely piled up. The young man sees this clearly. His is the difficult moral decision between Meiklejohn's questions "Is it right?" and "Does it pay?" [2]. It is in this area, again, that the college needs protection from the graduate schools *as they are now constituted*. Further examples of practice that belies preaching surround us. The problem is not easy to solve, but it is exigent. Let us teach so that what is right *will* pay.

But what I feel to be particularly important, since basic to these other problems, was discussed in part by Meiklejohn at the Experimental College Reunion [3]. He quoted Carl Sandburg's poem "Wilderness," the last stanza of which reads:

> O, I got a zoo, I got a menagerie, inside my ribs, under my bony head, under my red-valved heart —and I got something else: it is a man-child heart, a woman-child heart: it is a father and mother and lover: it came from God-Knows-Where: it is going to God-Knows-Where—For I am the keeper of the zoo: I say yes and no: I sing and kill and work: I am a pal of the world: I came from the wilderness.

Meiklejohn said:

> There are two very different ways of reading that poem, especially its last stanza. In one mood, Sandburg seems to hear the women and men of his time saying, "I came out of the Wilderness, and the Wil-

derness will not let me go." But in the other mood, the same women and men, facing the same facts, are saying, "I came from God-Knows-Where; I am going to God-Knows-Where; I am a pal of the world; for I am keeper of the Zoo; I say yes and no." And to this he might have added: "There are no yesses or noes in the Wilderness."

But what I am insisting, and have supported in Chapter 7 through Haskell's work, is that there *are* yesses and noes in the Wilderness. Yesses and noes permeate everything. This is suggested in Figure 7.2. A great and meaningful consistency pervades the universe, from the behaviors of atomic particles to that of nations.

This, then, is the point. It bears on conduct. One has to believe that what he does makes a difference: a difference to himself and to his community, and that he can say out of himself, "Yes" and "No". This takes us back to our premises.

In the long history of the human race we *have* learned certain things about living together. These have been codified in the principles of the Great Religions as codes of ethics. "Ethics, as a study of moral action, involves the most adequate possible understanding of the self, society, and culture, the heritage of moral principles and Christian life, and the technical data pertinent to particular decisions" says Paul Ramsay [4]. Here, it seems to me, we have by implication the basis for the premise of wholeness: that ethical principles emerge when the Humanities, Sciences, Technologies, and Philosophies are brought together in a connected whole. This has been, indeed, a burden of this book.

I do not mean to invoke some new Utopia. Chad Walsh has shown us the delusiveness of Utopias. What I want to do is to sensitize against the purveyors of dystopias who, knowingly or not, split man into his many functions. What is the meaning of the personal pronoun "I" when the fragmenters have labeled roles and function, and symbolized these with appropriate "hats": I_1, $I_2, \ldots, I_n$? "By weakening the sense of the individual identity," says Walsh, "they [the rulers of dystopias] make it more likely that the average man will merge his own frail identity with the social whole and cease to demand that he be called by a name instead of a number . . ." [5]. To show the uses of meaning to the person himself, in combating this fragmentation, has been my hope; to add this educational weapon to the others that might be grasped.

Perhaps the burden of this second point is that there are bases for belief which the student should be helped (as needed) to find—perhaps through the trials of doubt. Such belief should guide his actions, so that they are not inconsistent with his integrity.

My third point has to do with ambiguity, and I have said a good deal about this already, and wish only to suggest that this is an inherent property of the way things are, and must be lived with. I would not elevate it to a position of worship, for that would be stultifying in the end. One tries always to subdue the essential ambiguity of life by means of great organizing ideas which, based on evidence and reason, prevent one from being victimized at least in *that* direction. One may thus armor himself and subdue timidity "in the face of life's possibilities"—but this armor must not encapsulate him.

What, then, needs to be done? This book may be taken as an initial program. But I hope that it is clear that I do not prescribe for each teacher. I offer *an* approach. Each person, in his own style, may use what of it seems germane. He will have to invent and create his solutions. I have tried to offer firm premises and an occasional check list. Many colleges and universities are engaged in self-examination. There seems to be in some of them a very fine, open relation between all levels of the college. Much of the activity I have observed, however, seems to me on reflection to consist of instrumental changes and rearrangement of minutiae: changing from two semesters to two with a minimester between, or at the end; changing the grading system so that different symbols produce the same net result (as they have to, since discrimination of quality is an essence of education). In only a few places are the problems approached at a philosophical or a substantive level.

Following a suggestion of Haskell's, let the college be looked at as a cybernetic system. The input comprises the variables: students, faculty, administration, alumni, government (local and national), various contingencies, and much more. The output is changed behavior of students, faculty, and administration, all three of which are important, and only the first of which is generally recognized. The goal is persons whose education is advanced in a liberal sense, and who are motivated to continue to educate themselves. Seeing the whole, thinking of short- and long-range consequences, they become better stewards of their spaceship: persons who have developed a fiduciary attitude toward education and their responsibilities. The educational "entity" is in retroaction with its "habitat," the immediate community and the nation; and these influence it in a dynamic process.

The "governor" may comprise a committee, chaired by the president or academic dean, and made up of representatives of all the departments and of a few student organizations. Its purpose is twofold: to educate itself to find out what theoretical changes continually need to be made, and how to embody these in orderly action; and to maintain open channels of communication throughout the institution. The initial agenda of this body might comprise basically a study of the synthesis presented in Chapter 7, and an examination of course offerings with efforts to make them relevant to the students' lives such as might be based on Chapters 3 and 4.

How make a course relevant to the students' lives? If it is done, there should be no difficulty in maintaining both quantity and quality of course content. This is what I would suggest from my own experiences with intelligent and outspoken students. The teacher should express his world view (and he surely has one). If he believes that the whole man is one who "lives in three dimensions: the somatic, the mental, and the spiritual" (Frankl

[6]), that is, if he believes in the unity of body, mind, and spirit, he should say so, or indicate so by his behavior. A few comments at the end of a class period, tying things together—exposing implications—that is what helps. For what he teaches cannot but impinge on the physical part of his students' lives in some way. Man does not live by bread alone; but he does need "bread" to live. What he teaches always has mental components: the rational tools of symbol and construct, and the invariant-relations between constructs; the delights of intuitive understanding, coming whole; the irrational nudges of chance that, like any other deliverance of his brain, may be used or abused. What he teaches surely calls on that which makes us human beings: the "will-to-meaning" (Frankl) concerned with the actualization of values. The student lives in these three dimensions and is concerned with them. Any subject whatsoever may be made relevant to them explicitly or indirectly, and thus to his life. In his own style the teacher should make all these points of contact between human being and subject taught clear enough for the student to grasp and find meaning in what he is receiving, whether he agrees or not with its detailed premises.

Does the humanist student wonder why he is urged to study physical science? Then let us show him how this has been a powerful means of apprehending the world about us and controlling many of its phenomena. But not stop there. For we can point him in the direction of unified science (vestigially introduced in Chapter 7).

We can point out, and even illustrate by methods of thinking, that the mind of the science student is not somatically different from his. We can bring it home to him that as a steward of this Spaceship Earth (Boulding [7]) it behooves him not only to understand its working in general terms but to realize the powerful, pervasive logic that permeates every behavior, from atoms to cosmos. And we can help him to learn how to estimate consequences of the acts of people so that he can exercise his stewardship with wisdom—for people will respond to poetry and literature and song and art who will not even look at a scientific report, much less read it. And we can go further: we can tell him how scientific theory is responsive to the cultural milieu in which its inventor scientists live and grow up. Max Jammer, in an exhaustive study [8], says that without doubt Kierkegaard, "through his influence on Bohr," influenced the course of modern physical theory. So he is not without responsibility: indeed, as I have tried to show, his responsibility is enormous. We can call his attention to the values inherent in the scientist's activities. Every scientific investigation has moral import as the act of a person, and is based on beliefs: that there is order in the universe and that it can be found, or approximated; that the shots must be called as they are; and that special precautions must be taken not to be fooled by the duplicity of appearances. But this effort requires holistic science teaching.

Does the science or engineering student wonder

KNOWLEDGE, EXPERIENCE, AND ACTION

why he is asked to study literature, art, and history? Then let us show him that life is not all cognitive play with constructs, and with things that may be manipulated, but that interactions between people, struggles with one's own self, visions of past high and noble achievements of men and women, all weave together a subtle, complicated living pattern without which his science would lose its savor and become as dust. We can show him how much his knowledge is dependent on the spirit in which it is obtained, and on its cultural milieu; and how personal it finally is (Polanyi [9]). We can help him to see the consequences of his knowledge: how his attempts to penetrate the logic that pervades the universe may be used to make this Spaceship Earth a better place for his children, provided that to his science there is also assimilated humanity and compassion. These great qualities are brought to him primarily through home teaching, and later through the humanities: through great literature chosen with care and taught in understandable terms so that its beauty and qualitative precision of expression and high purposes are not lost in footnote hopping.

In the Preface to his *Idea of a University,* written over a hundred years ago (1852), Cardinal Newman wrote of certain desiderata of intellectual training [10]. These he lists:

the force, the steadiness, the comprehensiveness and the versatility of intellect, the command over our own powers, the instinctive just estimate of things as they pass before us, which sometimes indeed is a natural gift, but commonly is not gained without much effort and the exercise of years.

The "first step in intellectual training," he says,

is to impress upon a [student's] mind the idea of science, method, order, principle, and system; of rule and exception, of richness and harmony . . . to stimulate his powers into action in every practicable way, and to prevent a merely passive reception of images and ideas which in that case are likely to pass out of the mind as soon as they have entered it. Let him once gain this habit of method, of starting from fixed points, of making his ground good as he goes, of distinguishing what he knows from what he does not know, and I conceive he will be gradually initiated into the largest and truest philosophical views, and will feel nothing but impatience and disgust at the random theories and imposing sophistries and dashing paradoxes, which carry away halfformed and superficial intellects.

I believe that all these desiderata remain valid today, and I close by recalling them with a certain feeling of confidence. If all around us change presses in; if computers, automation, electronic music, the wizardry of strange molecules and psychotomimetic drugs, and so on, press in on us, we can still hold to certain educational verities. We can still teach ". . . the force, the steadiness, the comprehensiveness, and versatility of intellect, the command over our own powers, the instinctive just estimate of things as they pass before us. . ." And we can continue to find meaning in the "richness and harmony" of Knowledge, Experience, and Action: of Perceiving eyes, Enlightened minds, and Windowed hearts.

NOTES

1 Robert Rankin, in a lecture at the Danforth Foundation Workshop on the Liberal Arts, Colorado Springs, Summer 1962.

2 Alexander Meiklejohn, *Education Between Two Worlds* (Harper & Row, Publishers, New York, 1942), *cf.* p. 66.

3 Alexander Meiklejohn, Speech at the 1962 Experimental College Reunion, University of Wisconsin, June 8–10, 1962, pp. 19–26. [I am indebted to Mr. and Mrs. James A. Munro for calling this speech to my attention.]

4 Paul Ramsey, ed., *Faith and Ethics: The Theology of H. Richard Niebuhr* (Harper & Row, Publishers, New York, 1957), p. 126.

5 Chad Walsh, *From Utopia to Nightmare* (Harper & Row, Publishers, New York, 1962), p. 143.

6 Viktor E. Frankl, *The Doctor and the Soul: From Psychotherapy to Logotherapy* (Second expanded and revised edition; Alfred A. Knopf, Inc., New York, 1966).

7 Kenneth E. Boulding, in *Human Values on the Spaceship Earth* (National Council of Churches, New York, 1966).

8 Max Jammer, *The Conceptual Development of Quantum Mechanics* (McGraw-Hill Book Company, New York, 1966), *cf.* pp. 172 ff.

9 Michael Polanyi, *Personal Knowledge: Toward a Post-Critical Philosophy.* Harper Torchbooks (Harper & Row, Publishers, New York, 1964 [University of Chicago Press, Chicago, Ill., 1958, 1962]).

I have discussed some of the ideas about the college taken as a cybernetic system in "The University's Task: Wholeness," in *The Graduate Journal,* Spring, 1962; "The University-Community System—Self-Regulated Bearer of Meaning," in *General Systems,* 1966; "Cybernetics and Education," in *Ball State University Forum, 8*:3 (1967). See also "On Incipient Environmental Collapse," in *Bio-Science, 17*:878 (1967).

10 John Henry Cardinal Newman, *The Idea of a University* (Longmans, Green & Company, London, 1925).

Index